Jason Robards Remembered

Jason Robards Remembered

Essays and Recollections

THE EUGENE O'NEILL SOCIETY

Stephen A. Black, Zander Brietzke,
Jackson R. Bryer, *and* Sheila Hickey Garvey, *editors*

McFarland & Company, Inc., Publishers
Jefferson, North Carolina, and London

This book is published in association with the Eugene O'Neill Foundation–Tao House.

Front cover: Jason Robards at Tao House, 1989, when he accepted the first annual Tao House Award for his contribution to the American theatre. Used with the permission of the Eugene O'Neill Foundation–Tao House.

Frontispiece: Jason Robards at the grave of Blemie, O'Neill's dalmation, at the Tao House property. Used with the permission of the Eugene O'Neill Foundation–Tao House.

Opposite: Lois O'Connor Robards and Jason Robards, photographed at Monte Cristo Cottage, New London, in 1997 at a memorial service for Travis Bogard. Used with permission of the photographer, A. Vincent Scarano of New London.

Library of Congress Cataloguing-in-Publication Data

Jason Robards remembered : essays and recollections / The Eugene O'Neill
    Society / Stephen A. Black ... [et al.], editors.
       p.   cm.
    Includes bibliographical references and index.
    ISBN 0-7864-1356-5 (softcover : 50# alkaline paper) ∞
    1. Robards, Jason—Interviews.   2. Robards, Jason—Anecdotes.
I. Black, Stephen A. II. Eugene O'Neill Society.
PN2287.R62A5   2002
792'.028'092—dc21   2001008622

British Library cataloguing data are available

Manufactured in the United States of America

McFarland & Company, Inc., Publishers
  Box 611, Jefferson, North Carolina 28640
    www.mcfarlandpub.com

This book is dedicated by its editors
to Lois O'Connor Robards

Acknowledgments

In addition to the authors who contributed articles, and to other individuals mentioned in the Preface, we are happy to acknowledge the assistance of the following people: Ms. Rosemarie Germana of Dow, Jones & Co., Inc.; Thomas Lisanti of the New York Public Library; Tim McCanna of the Roundabout Theatre Company; Linda Matthews of A Cappella Books; Robert A. Richter of Connecticut College; David Seitz of the New York Times Co.; A. Vincent Scarano of New London, Connecticut; Sherry Picker of TimePix; Patricia Willis, Curator of American Literature at the Beinecke Library, Yale University; and Staci Wolfe of Polaris PR, Inc.

Contents

Acknowledgments	vi
Preface	1

PART ONE: INTERVIEWS AND ESSAYS

Yvonne Shafer, "Interviewing Jason Robards"	7
Deborah Merola, "An Interview with Jason Robards"	15
Michael Manheim, "Jason as Hickey, Jamie and Eugene"	22
Sheila Hickey Garvey, "Not for Profit"	27
Stephen A. Black, "On Jason Robards as O'Neill's Nietzschean Iceman"	40
Arthur Gelb, "Long Journey into Light"	49
Barbara Gelb, "Jason Jamie Robards Tyrone"	54
Edward L. Shaughnessy, "A Meeting with the Redoubtable Jason"	68
Edwin J. McDonough, "Quintero Directs Robards in *A Touch of the Poet*"	81
Shelia Hickey Garvey, "Recreating a Myth: *The Iceman Cometh* in Washington, D.C., 1985"	93

Madeline Smith and Richard Eaton, "Jason Robards:
    Crunching the Numbers"   103

Zander Brietzke, "O'Neill's Cry for Players"   112

PART TWO: MEMORIES AND TRIBUTES

George Beecroft Remembers *The Iceman Cometh*, 1956   119

Travis Bogard, "Presentation of the First Eugene O'Neill
    Foundation–Tao House Award"   122

Arvin Brown Remembers   129

Zoe Caldwell Remembers   131

Douglas Campbell Remembers   133

Wendy Cooper, "Jason Robards, Jr., and Eugene O'Neill's
    Tao House"   134

Blythe Danner Remembers   144

Richard Allan Davison, Memories of "Jason Robards, Jr.,
    Actor's Actor"   146

Robert Einenkel, "A Movie Struck Young Man Discovers
    Theater"   151

Sheila Hickey Garvey, "For Jason 'Jamie' Robards"   153

George Grizzard Remembers   158

A. R. Gurney Remembers   161

Shirley Knight Remembers   163

Daniel Larner Remembers   164

Paul Libin, "Jason Owned the House"   166

Lois McDonald Remembers   169

Theodore Mann Remembers   171

Joe Morgenstern, "Goodbye, Tumbleweed"   176

Sally Thomas Pavetti, "He Never Turned Me Down" 179

Christopher Plummer Remembers 182

Margaret and Ralph Ranald Remember 185

The Roundabout Theatre, "Remembering Jason Robards, 1922–2000" 187

Charles Saydah, "Jason Robards 1922–2000" 189

Kevin Spacey, "An Example, a Mentor, an Actor Above All" 191

Eli Wallach Remembers 195

Appendix: Jason Robards' Performances in Theatre, Film and Television 199

Index 205

J R, 1920–2000

He took within himself such pains
    as playwrights know
of being only human in the world.
He lived them out on stage
(or so it seems)
    that we might know,
and forgive ourselves.
He showed us that
(as O'Neill once wrote)
"We are as God made us.
    God help us."

S.A.B.

Preface

We in the Eugene O'Neill Society have much to be thankful for. For most of us, our meetings and conventions have given us, from time to time, the rare chance to hear some of the people who had created the great O'Neill productions talk about their work on stage. We were especially lucky to have with us on a few occasions Jason Robards, who was willing and able to speak with some candor about his work in the late O'Neill plays. Now he is gone. We write in celebration of his life.

The interviews and essays in Part One of the book give accounts of an actor seen from the point of view of the audience. They begin with accounts of two interviews with Jason, in which we hear him speaking of his life, of his career as an actor, and of O'Neill and his plays. Also in Part One, O'Neill scholars try to find objective bases for the assumption we make that Jason's performances of O'Neill were essential to the effect the late plays have had on us. We believe that the revival of O'Neill's public reputation that began in 1956 can be directly traced to the production directed by José Quintero that year of *The Iceman Cometh* in an Off Broadway theatre, the Circle in the Square, in which Robards played the salesman Hickey. Several of us believe that Jason showed the world how O'Neill's plays work, on stage and on the page, and we write about what we think he taught us about watching or reading the plays. The essays are arranged approximately in the order of the Robards–Quintero productions of the late O'Neill plays: *Iceman* and *Long Day's Journey Into Night* (1956–57), *A Moon for the Misbegotten* (1973–74), and *A Touch of the Poet* (1977–78).

1

Part Two consists mostly of accounts by people who knew Jason as a friend or colleague, or who had some encounter with him that remains important in their memories. The contributions are arranged alphabetically. Most are brief and deeply subjective. Jason was loved by many of the people who knew him or met him.

Almost all of the memoirs by friends show Jason telling stories. He was a great storyteller, who enjoyed retelling his stories. We hear multiple recollections of some of the stories and get a notion of why Jason told the stories over and over. The stories that Jason liked to tell show us something about him and his ways with his friends.

Not all accounts of Jason in Part Two are by friends or theatrical colleagues. A couple are ceremonious. Wendy Cooper, president of the Eugene O'Neill Foundation–Tao House, made available to us the presentation speech given by the late O'Neill scholar Travis Bogard when Jason was awarded the first Tao House Award for his Contribution to the American Theatre. Wendy Cooper also gives her personal recollections of visits Jason made to Tao House, and recalls some of Jason's many works that helped save O'Neill's Bay Area house and place it under the protection of the National Parks Service.

Several give the memories of strangers who happened to see him in a play and were deeply affected, and who, perhaps, caught some glimpse of the man behind the actor. Three are formal obituaries published in newspapers and magazines. (Details of the prior publication of any works being reprinted in this volume are given in headnotes in the body of the book.)

Our book began its life the day after Jason Robards passed away, December 26, 2000. We of the O'Neill Society, like the rest of America, immediately knew that we had lost a very good friend, and that we should find a way to mark his passing. The Board of the O'Neill Society agreed that we should try to make a book of tributes and other essays that expressed our debt to Jason, and our sense of loss at his passing. We had originally hoped to get the book out within a year. The four of us named as editors have collaborated in gathering tributes from Jason's friends and from strangers, in arranging for some essays to be reprinted, and in editing, organizing, typing the contributions into computer files, and performing the many other chores necessary to prepare a manuscript for a publisher. Zander Brietzke did an enormous amount of typing, editing, and inquiring about permissions to reprint previously published work, and he obtained the two remarkable photos of the *Long Day's Journey* cast and of Colleen Dewhurst and Jason in *A Moon for the Misbegotten*. Diane Schinnerer, secretary-treasurer of the Eugene O'Neill Society, has helped in numerous ways throughout our work, too many ways to specify, but it must be mentioned that she enabled us to use photos from the Tao House collection. Lois McDonald sent us several of A. Vincent Scarano's fine photos of Jason at Monte Cristo Cottage, at The Eugene O'Neill Theater Center and at Connecticut College; and Mr. Scarano gave us permission to print them here. Robert Franklin of McFarland & Company, Inc., Publishers, a longtime friend of O'Neill, offered to drop everything else to get the manuscript published as soon as we could get it to him, to help us honor Jason Robards in a timely way. Above all, we thank our contributors for the essays published here.

Many of us recall several conferences at Suffolk University in Boston which were organized by our host, Frederick Wilkins, a founding member of the Society, and founding editor of *The Eugene O'Neill Review*. Fred arranged at various times for Jason Robards and José Quintero to speak about performing O'Neill. We heard many of the stories that are told and retold by contributors to this book, and because they are such good stories, they seem to grow with the repetition, rather than grow stale.

I will retell two of the stories, one that is not told elsewhere in the book, and the other because it has particular relevance to me as someone who taught students to read O'Neill's plays for more than thirty years. The latter story is of Jason preparing himself to play Hickey in 1956. He said, approximately, that when he began studying *Iceman*, "I did what any actor does; before I read the play, I went through the book and crossed out all the stage directions with a heavy pencil. I read and reread the play, and Hickey wasn't making sense to me. Finally, it occurred to me that I needed to know what was in the stage directions. I got a good eraser and erased the marks I had made and read it again, and finally I began to understand the play."

Many people have said over the years that O'Neill wrote as if he wanted to be a novelist rather than a playwright, and have cited as evidence the very detailed character descriptions and stage directions. Perhaps it is so or perhaps he had to visualize very specifically the scenes he was imagining. Whatever the reason, it seems clear that a reader learns about O'Neill's characters as one learns about the characters in a novel, and part of that is in the stage directions. The stage directions have been criticized by actors who plausibly say that one cannot be expected to show a character, for example, with an expression "no longer self-assured ... [but instead] uneasy, baffled, resentful ... [with] the stubborn set of an obsessed determination" as Hickey is described at his entrance in Act 4. O'Neill was evidently not telling the actor what to do. He apparently assumed that actors would learn about their characters as he himself learned about characters in a novel; he apparently assumed the actors would read the play, including the stage directions, as one reads a novel. Robards felt that when he had read the whole play, including the stage directions, he knew not what the actor was asked to do, but what the character was thinking and feeling as he spoke. For Jason that was enough. If the actor understood intuitively what the character thought and felt, he would find ways to express it. The story tells us much that is valuable, both for readers and for directors and actors.

The other story went something like this. During the war Jason had gone into the ship's library and picked up a book, he said, because the title, *Strange Interlude*, made him think "it might be a dirty book." The book introduced him to O'Neill and he read more O'Neill plays and began to think that he might want to be an actor after all, even though the profession had not treated his father kindly. Later, when he was out of the Navy and studying acting in New York, he had gone to see *The Iceman Cometh* with some of his fellow students. He found something in the play that affected him; he went back to see it a second time, after the actor playing Hickey had dropped out of the show and been replaced. That time the play moved him deeply. When it was finished, he said, he walked up the aisle toward the lobby in a fog. As he neared the last row of seats, someone whispered to him, "Look: there's O'Neill." Sure enough, there sat O'Neill. Ever since then, Robards said, I've been glad to be able to say to myself, "I was once in the same room as O'Neill." Robards made many of us in the O'Neill Society glad to be able to say, "I was once in the same room as Jason Robards."

Stephen A. Black
President, The Eugene O'Neill Society, 2000–2001
December 2001

PART ONE
Interviews and Essays

Jason Robards speaks at Connecticut College, April, 2000, when the College awarded honorary degrees to Arthur and Barbara Gelb. Used by the kind permission of the photographer, A. Vincent Scarano, and Connecticut College.

Interviewing Jason Robards

by Yvonne Shafer

> Yvonne Shafer lives on Staten Island and teaches at St. John's University. Her most recent book is *Performing O'Neill: Conversations with Actors and Directors* (St. Martin's Press, 2000), from which all quotations in the following essay are taken.

Interviewing Edward Petherbridge about his experience in *Strange Interlude* was so enlightening and such fun that I decided to do a book about performing O'Neill. Michael Flamini, my editor at St. Martin's Press, and I agreed immediately that such a book would hinge on the possibility of getting an interview with Jason Robards. I wrote directly to him, unaware that he was at that time in the hospital, very ill. By the time of the Tony Awards, he was well enough to make a presentation and he also spoke at the memorial service for José Quintero. By that time, I had had the pleasure of interviewing Fritz Weaver and Fritz offered to call Jason to say hello and to encourage him to let me do an interview. Almost immediately, I came home to hear something on my message machine which thrilled me: that wonderful, familiar voice saying hello, and saying he would call again. We quickly set up a date for me to visit him at his home in Connecticut in June 1999.

Every interview is different; some actors just take off and start telling stories and others give surprising answers such as, "No, I never played that," or "No," with nothing to follow. As I had not met Jason and only knew the events in his life and the roles he chose to play, I was quite unprepared for the joyous, delightful person I would interview. As I drove in through the gates to the gorgeous home overlooking Long Island Sound, I saw him standing in the doorway wearing khaki trousers and a yellow tennis shirt with a big smile on his face. When I set up not one, but two, tape recorders as a buttress against any possible failure, he grinned and said, "One never knows, do one?"

During the two-hour interview I was most impressed by many qualities. The first was his infectious, truly irrepressible sense of humor. Whatever subject came up, he had a funny story about it. When he played Hickey there was no offstage space in the old Circle in the Square, so he waited for his last entrance and the speech which makes such a tremendous demand on the actor on a bench in Sheridan Square. Every once in a while he would go put his ear to the door to see how far along the actors were. He could have gone on and on with funny stories such as that of Steve McQueen stopping by and engaging him in a conversation about trying out for *Stalag 17* just minutes before his entrance. He was equally funny talking about his struggle to make ends meet before he played that role by acting on the radio, being a stage manager, working as a typist-secretary and teaching ("I didn't know anything, but I taught"). He laughed with delight as he remembered his meeting with Carlotta Monterey at lunch. He and Quintero were all spiffed up and determined to be on their best behavior: no liquor! Then he said that they noticed that Mrs. O'Neill's drink—a "Carlotta Monterey"—seemed to be heightening her spirits and they decided to try it out, thus falling off the wagon with delightful results. One of his enthusiasms was playing in *Hughie*, which he played off and on with Jack Dodson for thirty-two years. He talked about performing in San Francisco one evening after having spoken to Travis Bogard's students at Berkeley that afternoon. The students had been very responsive and had come to see the performance. There was a sort of alley which ran between the Geary Theatre and the theatre they were in. Jason said, "When Jack and I came out, the whole ground was covered with rose petals! I said, 'What the hell is this?' and Jack said, 'I don't know—let's get a drink!' It was the students who had done it" (132).

His own sense of humor was important in his performances of O'Neill. To many readers and actors, O'Neill is totally serious, even grim. Jason loved the comedy in O'Neill. Even as a student he recognized one of the problems in the original production of *The Iceman Cometh*. He said, "It was like looking at *The Lower Depths* forever—there wasn't anything, comedy or anything, it was just 'bluuh'" (122). He spoke at length about the difference in approach when Quintero directed it, particularly in terms of the comedy. In his audition he read the long speech at the end which seemed to impress Quintero who then told him to do something funny. "Some part from the beginning, wanted me to play funny. Wanted to see if I could be funny. So I read some stuff up front, in the early part of the play where he's joyful" (125). By six that evening Quintero had called to tell him he had the role. In describing the performances he recalled that he rarely ever heard such laughter as during the first act of *The Iceman Cometh*. (One should recall that he played in many comedies including *A Thousand Clowns*.) He said that the entire first act has great comic pieces of writing, that O'Neill built a bubble which slowly deflated as the play went on. He also talked about the delight of playing the comedy in *Ah, Wilderness!* with Colleen Dewhurst in repertory with *Long Day's Journey Into Night*. He said that he loved O'Neill's comedy, "Everybody did," and that playing the two plays in repertory in 1998 was "absolutely heaven because there was the same play, opposite sides of the coin" (146).

Another impressive thing was his memory. I honestly think that he had the best memory of any person I have ever met in my life. This interview took place when he was 77 years old and had performed in dozens of plays and theatres. Without a moment's hesitation, when I mentioned a production, he would tell me some particulars about one of the shows in which he had performed, giving the number of seats in the house, the length of time, and the year he played it, and often how much profit there was and what was done with it. His phenomenal memory was a great help to him in playing O'Neill's roles, naturally. Generous in spirit, he had little negative to say about James Barton's failure to learn the lines for the original *Iceman* production, but spoke rather of the impact the actor's face—almost a mask of death—made on him. That image haunted him from the time he saw the play as a student at the American Academy of Dramatic Arts and he was truly driven to play the role of Hickey. He told me that he always got a pretty good idea of some of the longer speeches before he began rehearsals—not like Fredric March who really tried to learn the whole role before he began rehearsals—but just a good sense of the speeches.

One of his most unique stories had to do with making a film in Colorado. The filming lasted for six months and most of the company stayed near Canon City, driving 56 miles each way every day to and from the shooting location. He chose to live in a little summer cabin, with one room and a couple of sleeping areas. He said the cabin was so small that he could get the phone from any part—just reach out. Here he decided to pass the long winter evenings writing out the entire script of *A Touch of the Poet* in which he would perform when the film was completed. He filled page after page with the text, writing by hand as O'Neill had done. And after he had written out the whole play, he started learning it. So when rehearsals began, he had not learned the dialogue with the others, but had a good grip on the long speeches.

His warmth and generosity were also evident throughout both interviews. This was particularly important to me as he spent about two hours with me in July, despite his problems with his health and the professional obligations he had. (He was finishing *Magnolia* which had been postponed by his illness.) He then allowed me to come back for two hours more in August. During the interviews his wife, Lois, and his son, Jake, came in and his love and affection for them was marvelous to see. He also spoke of his love for the house and the view of the Sound. We sat in an enormous room with glass all along one side, the room painted all light colors, the sunlight pouring in, and fresh flowers in vases. When I gave him a basket of fresh fruit, he was delighted and called his wife to come in and see it, commenting that it looked like a still life painting. When I asked him what he felt made the close connection in his mind with O'Neill, his answer was a surprise. He told me that he just loved the music of O'Neill's time—the same music O'Neill used many times in the plays.

It was also interesting to hear of Jason's love for his father who was an actor. His father had acted on the stage, but went to Hollywood in the twenties, and Jason felt he had ruined his career by remaining there. (It's interesting that O'Neill often expressed the opinion that an actor had been very good, but had been ruined by acting in Hollywood.) Jason described his father as a handsome man with a wonderful voice. As a young man, Jason was uncertain of what to do with his life, so he spent seven years in the navy—his youthful experience providing another parallel with O'Neill. When he thought about acting, his father advised him to go to the American Academy of Dramatic Arts as he had done in 1910. Jason was pleased by the fact that he studied with some of the same teachers as his father had. He described his father's strange experience in seeing *Long Day's Journey Into Night*. His father had been blinded by cataracts for eight or nine years and had only recently had an operation so that he could see again. When he came to the performance, the color and the experience of seeing again stunned him. He asked if he could sit in the wings the next night and just listen to it. Fredric March, with whom Jason's father had acted, said of course he could. An interesting comment Jason made was that his father loved the play: "You know it was about an actor father, an actor's son, a mother vague and distant, as my mother was. Not on drugs, but distant from the family. You know it was very parallel in a lot of ways" (140). Jason was reluctant to say too much about his father because he wanted to write a book about him. That he didn't live long enough to write it is a real sorrow.

Jason loved his father and also loved Fredric March as a father figure. He felt that he was a superb actor and that the great success of *Long Day's Journey Into Night* lay in part in March's modest approach to acting and his eagerness to take direction and learn. Jason said that even when he played the role of the father, he could still hear "Freddie's" voice. One of the actors at Jason's memorial service said that he had asked Jason how he had learned to act and he said by sitting in the wings and watching Fredric March.

His generosity of spirit and warmth was also revealed by his comments about other actors and directors, particularly Quintero. He was openly generous in other ways, too. For example, when he and Dodson played *Hughie* in San Francisco, they gave the money to pay part of the mortgage for Tao House and later gave the total profits of the run to it as well. When Trinity Rep in Providence was in financial difficulties, he and Dodson performed the play as the season opener to help them "get some dough in there" (133). They also performed the play for various schools and charities. Although he could laugh at his own terrible problems with alcohol, he viewed alcoholism seriously and gave his time to do work for the Mayo Clinic in connection with the disease. He traveled around the country performing a monologue from *Iceman* for doctors. Then he worked for a program called Insight, in which he performed to clarify problems of denial and enablement in drinking. He and Teresa Wright and his son Sam did scenes from *Long Day's Journey Into Night* illustrating alcohol and drugs issues in family dynamics for an audience of 14,000 in San Francisco.

Such acts of generosity continued throughout his career, even as he was compelled to go to Hollywood, which he called "the Land of the Living Dead," to make "alimony movies." At the February 2001 memorial for Jason, George Grizzard quoted him about those and other comments he made about Hollywood which, he said, drove Jason's agent crazy. Despite his ironic comments, his work in Hollywood was typical of his acting on the stage: totally professional and never arrogant or high hat. Another speaker at the memorial was *Magnolia* director Paul Thomas Anderson, who said that Jason told him he wanted suggestions and line readings and that the director didn't need to pussyfoot around as he wanted all the help he could get.

When he discussed acting with me, he revealed his respect for it, his serious attitude about theatre, and his reverence for O'Neill, but at the same time dismissed much of the theorizing about acting as self-indulgent. When I made reference to the difficulty some actors would have experienced sitting outside the theatre on a public bench before an emotional scene instead of getting into character in a private place, he laughed and said, "No, I don't do all that crap—where did that come from? It was Lee Strasberg and the lousy Method" (127). Again, speaking of the delving into the subconscious and memory of emotion, he said, "I don't believe in all that crap. Excuse me, but that's something that if you want, go into analysis. It has nothing to do with acting" (142). When he spoke of acting O'Neill, he said it was really simple because O'Neill wrote so well. "I thought it was as easy as walking and looking at a map and saying you turn right at that corner and go up that street, come down that little alley there and you go in" (142). He was, of course, over-simplifying, but he was essentially an intuitive actor, which was one reason he worked so well with José Quintero, whose approach was also intuitive. Working with a director on stage or in film, Jason would often ask, "May I try something?" and would then, with some gesture, movement, or surprising line delivery, create a great moment and a memorable scene. Matthew Broderick was one of the many actors at the memorial service who spoke of how much he learned about acting from watching Jason. Kevin Spacey talked about the graciousness of the great actor to a younger actor about to play the roles he had made famous. Introduced by Colleen Dewhurst, Jason (aware that Spacey was to play Jamie) said of O'Neill, "Be good to him. He was good to me." Spacey also expressed the great respect actors of all types had for Jason, concluding, "He was the last of a breed of actors who dedicated themselves to a life in the theatre. Without asking for the role, he was our elder statesman."

A major quality in Jason's acting was the exhilaration and energy he exuded even in ordinary conversation. When he began the rigorous rehearsals for *Long Day's Journey Into Night,* he was performing *The Iceman Cometh* at night. He continued this exhausting regime for many weeks, but finally, laughing as he recalled it, he told Quintero he would have to get somebody else to play in *Iceman.* When he was in *Long Day's Journey,* he was so exhilarated by the role that he stayed up very late every night, wanting to keep the mood going. He also did other professional things after the performance: "Sometimes I'd play Jamie and then go to a symposium and do Hickey's big speech. I'd tell Freddie that and he'd just laugh" (131). When he played *Hughie,* he performed twelve times a week. When I commented that he would have performed it double on Sunday, he laughed his wonderful big laugh and said, "Double ones! I'd do three. I'd do a matinee and early evening and a late evening" (135). When he performed the two O'Neill plays in repertory with Colleen Dewhurst, they often did a matinee and an evening performance of the two demanding plays with only an hour in between: "We'd send out for sandwiches, eat them and go back out again" (135). When I asked him if he found all that wearing, he said no, but that sometimes he felt that he might not hit all the high points in an evening performance after having acted all afternoon, "But then, during the production, as it went on, I'd feel this hand on my back, pushing me, and I'd get fired up, and I think that was O'Neill pushing me" (134).

In October 2000, there was a conference on O'Neill at the Eugene O'Neill Theater Center in Waterford, Connecticut, which concluded with a tribute to Jason. Ted Mann was there and spoke about their work together on O'Neill's plays. George White gave a speech honoring

Jason, and pulled off the cover of a copy of the statue of O'Neill which is on a rock by the New London Harbor. At the sight of it, Jason was very moved. Tears ran down his cheeks and he said, "I owe my career to O'Neill, I owe my life to O'Neill." Seeing the three men who had contributed so much to O'Neill's present reputation and popularity, I wondered if I would ever see all of them together again and the tears were rolling down my cheeks.

The opportunity to interview Jason afforded me the chance to learn a great deal about him and about O'Neill, but it also afforded me the chance to share the warmth and love of life of a wonderful actor. He played so many O'Neill roles that his life was inextricably mixed with that of our greatest tragic playwright. Yet he loved to laugh, especially at himself. When I asked him if he had not wanted to play other O'Neill roles, he said that Natasha Richardson had begged him to play in "*Anna Christie*" with Liam and herself, but he had refused. "It's too melodramatic for me. I hate the play; and then I saw them and they were magnificent. [Laughing] And then I thought, 'Gee, I wish I had done it.' But that's O'Neill—it really works" (149).

From the beginning of the work on *Performing O'Neill*, I had decided to dedicate the book to Jason, to thank him for all the wonderful performances. He was a great man on the stage and off the stage as well; one of those of whom we can say, "We'll never see his like again."

An Interview with Jason Robards

by Deborah Merola

Deborah Merola is Associate Professor of Theatre at Hartwick College, Oneonta, N.Y. The following is excerpted from an interview that took place on October 5, 1985, at the Lunt-Fontanne Theatre in New York, where Jason Robards was performing in *The Iceman Cometh*.

Merola. I've heard that you've become a consultant to the Mayo Clinic on alcoholism. How did that happen?

Robards. I was called by the Mayo Clinic, a woman named Mary Adams Martin, who runs an outpatient clinic on alcoholism and drug abuse for the Mayo Clinic. And she said, "An interesting thing happened. We counsel families and people that have this trouble, and their families. We lecture them about 'denial' and 'enable' and all these terms in booze and drugs and things." I made a record for Columbia Records of the monologue. They asked me to do four excerpts of O'Neill's stuff, which I did. I didn't do them very well. One guy doing that is not good, you know. But the monologue, or this narrative of Evelyn, at least, was there. She said, "We played that audio, just played it over speakers to these people, and they immediately identified." I later did it on *20/20*. Did you see that *20/20*?

15

Merola. I didn't see that. I didn't know about that.

Robards. Where I did it with the alcoholics. Well, you ought to get a copy of it. ABC, *20/20.* You don't see much of the play, but at least it opens a discussion about alcohol and drugs. Well, I had never realized it was a teaching tool until Mary made this discovery.

Merola. That would surprise me, because it's pretty horrendous—the contents.

Robards. It's one of the great teaching tools there is. I find this. Now I use it, it's over at Pace Medical Service, which is another alcohol treatment center down here in New York. They have a tape of that program we did on denial. I go with two doctors and myself and a moderator, and we go all over the country for this. So I have been doing... We don't go a lot, I mean, maybe once, two times a year.

Merola. So it's something that you do?

Robards. In Dallas it played to 6,000 doctors. We played Washington, and Atlanta and Minneapolis and San Francisco, doing this program on denial. Now, and another thing, this is very interesting, that's been added. Helen Hayes did a thing on aging, the same thing. She did *Victoria Regina.* Then Kathy Bates did suicide, she did *'night, Mother.* And then Sam Robards and I, and Teresa Wright, and that other girl who was here, we did scenes from *Long Day's Journey* on the effect in a family of drug abuse, what happens to the members of this family. Sam, my son, played Edmund, I played Tyrone, Teresa was the mother, and the girl was the maid. Then she does the scene with the maid and the drugs, then we do the...

Merola. You'd have the discussion—

Robards. And then the whole thing, yeah. It's fascinating, and it's a teaching tool.

Merola. And it's healing.

Robards. You see, here's O'Neill, literature used in a wonderful sense. That's where... I don't mean to connect that with this play even, but it's just to show you that somewhere, it hasn't been just a spur of the moment decision. There was something in the head about doing it again. I said, "We've got to do the damn—We should do the play." I want to play Larry, I thought, now, I want to play Larry. I've always wanted to play Larry [in *The Iceman Cometh*].

Merola. Yes, that would be interesting.

Robards. But they didn't want me to play Larry, so I have to play Hickey again.

Merola. Why do you want to play Larry?

Robards. That's the tragic hero of the play, that's the true tragic—that's the true hero. Hickey is an outsider. He's not even in the play, he just comes in. The play is the hope in his group. Hickey and Parritt are outsiders, they're sober murderers.

Merola. Do you think Larry gets sold a bill of goods?

Robards. No.

Merola. Do you think he gets sold the real thing?

Robards. Sold a bill of goods? No, Larry is—he's denying a lot of stuff.

Merola. But he says he's the only convert to death.

Robards. We all gotta go, you know. When you gotta go, you gotta go. [Laughter]

Merola. I just saw *Iceman* again this afternoon, and I was thinking of the comfort left to Larry, and... Well he does give comfort, he puts Parritt out of his misery. But I'm never quite sure if Hickey—

Robards. He's a killer...

Merola. I'm never quite sure whether he—

Robards. Larry kills.

Merola. Uh-huh.

Robards. He kills for love. Again the same thing. He loved Rosa Parritt.

Merola. But do you think he's—

Robards. Desperately loved her. It doesn't come out in this production, but that's what's behind it. You see Myron McCormick? [Larry Slade in the 1960 *Play of the Week* TV Production. Conrad Bains was Larry Slade in the 1956 revival.]

Merola. Yes.

Robards. Now you know what Larry's about.

Merola. Yes.

Robards. That was one of the most brilliant performances I've ever seen.

Merola. Yes.

Robards. Myron's, yes. I couldn't look at it, it made me cry. He knew. He knew. And that's what this play's about.

Merola. Is Larry no better than Hickey, then?

Robards. Is he no better... What?

Merola. Yeah. I mean, if they both...

Robards. No, they're both sort of fine... They're not criminals or murderers or anything. They're just guys that are screwed up with love. They don't know how to handle love.

Merola. Do you know, I think audiences, too, in that same way, never quite figure *Iceman* out. Maybe it's such a great play that it doesn't figure out.

Robards. Listen, let them. I don't try to figure it out. I let them all have whatever they see in it. Like Anne Jackson saw it every night for two weeks and found something new in it.

Merola. Yes. I find something new in it all the time, too.

Robards. And she said it's one of the most fascinating plays. This is when we did that on PBS.

Merola. Do you know, it's because it's complex. Like the scene when Harry goes out, and Rocky goes over to the window to watch and the audience is pulling two different ways. I think the audience is real shocked to hear that Hickey won't go out with Hope. It doesn't seem kind. And when we hear that Hickey knew all along, and I think a part of the audience is pulling for Rocky at that point in time, just like a part of us pulls for different people.

Robards. Oh, well, yeah. He always… No. You can't pull for Hickey all the time.

Merola. But sometimes I'm not sure that Hickey isn't malevolent, isn't evil.

Robards. Well, I mean, that's for you to read. I can't play that.

Merola. No, I know.

Robards. It may come out that way, but I don't play evil. I gotta play help all the way through, help, help, help, help. See, that's all you can do. And that's what makes Hickey run into himself, when they can't pick it up. O'Neill says here, "His beaming expression is one of triumphant accomplishment." Not malevolent. Hickey is so happy that he has got this whole group down there on that morning—this is the third act—to go out. There they all are. This is what he's tried for, they're finally going to face themselves, and it's wonderful for him.

Merola. In this production it plays like a great comedy. I mean people are laughing a lot and people are really happy on a certain level.

Robards. Always did. Yeah, it always did.

Merola. I guess I haven't heard it with an audience. I was sitting there Thursday night and I was surprised at how—

Robards. Oh, it's funny, it's very funny.

Merola. I knew sections were funny, but I was really—

Robards. It's not comedy, jokes or anything, that carries him through. You gotta carry that. Hickey claps Hope on the back, still he's chuckling, laughing, all the way through. Amused, you know. It was a great act, he's amused. You see, it isn't some malevolent thing, and it's only when it gets away from him we see how far it goes. He doesn't even talk about his wife until we get over here, and Hugo, the next to the last speech of the play, starts going crazy, and talks about blood and death—that "always there is blood beneath the willow trees," I hate it, and he sobs. Crazy, crazy talk. And Hickey looks to everybody, and all this accumulation of what Larry meant. That's when he says he's beginning to worry. I can't play anything but, "It's gonna work..." Make believe it's gonna work.

Merola. Yes, I understand about the playing of it.

Robards. So, if you read he's malevolent, that's all right. If they say he's more malevolent, I don't feel right. I don't feel that he should be more malevolent. I don't think he's very—

Merola. No, I don't think it should play that way either.

Robards. And it plays that way sometimes, and that's because... I don't know what I was doing. I was young I didn't know what I was doing. Younger.

Merola. I just kind of wonder, finally, in terms of the meaning of the play itself—

Robards. Larry was a terrible guy, I mean, to say, "Look, we all know you found her [shacked up with the iceman]. Don't tell us." That's a terrible thing to say.

Merola. I know we've got to end pretty soon. I wanted to ask you if there's anything that you do respect in terms of the criticism, or in terms of reviews, or...

Robards. No, reviews, no. I haven't even read any reviews.

Merola. Is there anything in the biographies that you ever read?

Robards. I read some, yes. You know, I've read Lou Sheaffer and Barbara Gelb, Barbara and Arthur's book. But Lou's book reads like a novel almost, it's so wonderful.

Merola. Yes, it's a great book.

Robards. And Barbara, and that's history. But I think Travis's book was very fascinating, very fascinating. I liked all that stuff about the cycle, that was very, very interesting. But I don't... You mean as far as an actor? I don't... I thought that twentieth century thing on *The Iceman Cometh* was one of the worst pieces of shit I've ever read.

Merola. It's too literary?

Robards. Everybody... Eric Bentley always hated José and I, anyway. I mean, that was back in the Circle days.

Merola. And he hated O'Neill too.

Robards. He hated O'Neill... But what I'm trying to say is that I found the book was just so pretentious with all this stuff. Who are they talking about? This play is meant to be—just what it's doing now. Whether this is good or bad, if people want to see it or not, that'll come and go. But it must be done, it must not have anything but be done.

Merola. Oh, I think it's fine. I think it's wonderful.

Robards. It should be done a lot. Like Shakespeare, you do a lot of *Henry V*'s and you do *Hamlet*s and you do this and you do that. And you should do *Henry IV, Part I*, you should do this a lot. It should be part of repertory, it should be tried.

Merola. This idea of repertory was partly what I was getting at when I was talking about—

Robards. This should be played about three times a week.

Merola. Uh-huh. Because O'Neill talked about having a repertory company, and it would be wonderful to see... That's what I was talking about the James O'Neill role. I mean, it's as simple as, say, putting *Ah, Wilderness!* and *Long Day's Journey Into Night* against each other, or putting *A Touch of the Poet* and *The Iceman Cometh* against each other. Not that you have to make direct comparisons, those are tiresome, but there is some resonance, there is some way that words come back, that images come back, just like the train, like the way the trains... And it begins to accumulate a kind of richness.

Robards. The train in—

Merola. The train in so many things. I mean the train in *Iceman* where Hickey gets, when he tells Evelyn that he picked up venereal disease from drinking cups on trains. Of course the train for Jamie, with the whore. I just think it would be wonderful for people to—[interruption]. Well I should probably end, because I've taken up a tremendous amount of your time. I appreciate it.

Jason as Hickey, Jamie and Eugene

by Michael Manheim

Michael Manheim, a former President of the Eugene O'Neill Society, wrote *Eugene O'Neill: A New Language of Kinship* (Syracuse University Press, 1982) and edited *The Cambridge Companion to Eugene O'Neill* (Cambridge University Press, 1998).

I had the good fortune to see all but one of Jason's O'Neill performances. I saw him as Hickey in the Quintero/Mann production of *Iceman* in 1956 and the television version of that production; as Jamie in the Quintero *Long Day's Journey* in 1956 and the Sidney Lumet film in 1962; as Jim Tyrone in the Quintero *Moon for the Misbegotten* in 1974 and the television version of that production; as James Tyrone, Sr., in Jason's own production of *Long Day's Journey* in Ann Arbor (with Zoe Caldwell as Mary) in the late 1970s; and as Hickey again in the Quintero production of *Iceman* in 1985. We had tickets for José Quintero's *Long Day's Journey* with Jason and Colleen in the late 1980s, but that production was closed before we could get there. I also own his recorded reading of Erie Smith in *Hughie*. I keep imagining I saw him as Billy Brown in *The Great God Brown* somewhere along the way, but that must have been a production of my dreams. (I can really see him in the role.) Along with many others, I see Jason as not only the quintessential (with the pun on Quintero intended) O'Neill performer, but among those chiefly responsible for O'Neill's belated recognition as one of the master dramatists of the 20th century.

Jason's earlier interpretation of Hickey may have been key in establishing O'Neill's reputation for the ages, but one wonders what José Quintero and Ted Mann could have had in mind when they selected him, a then unknown young actor, for the role. In the text, O'Neill describes Hickey as follows:

> He is about fifty, a little under medium height, with a stout, roly-poly figure. His face is round and smooth and big-boyish with bright blue eyes, a button nose, a small, pursed mouth. His head is bald except for a fringe of hair around his temples and the back of his head. His face is fixed in a salesman's winning smile of self-confident affability and hearty good fellowship.

Jason was around 33 or 34 when he was cast for the role. He was around medium height, with a thin, almost gaunt-looking figure. His face was lean and craggy, with an aquiline nose and a wide-ish mouth. And I would have to call his a nervous affability, the winning quality always somewhat forced. Ronald Wainscott calls it "hard-edged" and "anxiety-ridden."[1] Surely there were actors Quintero and Mann looked at that came closer to O'Neill's description of Hickey. Was it just Jason's enthusiastic determination to get the role that convinced them, as has been suggested?[2]

Other interpreters of the role have come closer to O'Neill's description. James Barton, from his picture as the original Hickey in the 1946 Theatre Guild production, came close. And Lee Marvin in John Frankenheimer's film production of the early 1970s comes closer still. Marvin's overall demeanor seems based precisely on what O'Neill says. Yet, for a variety of reasons, Barton apparently failed in the role.[3] And I personally found Marvin's interpretation by far the weakest feature of an otherwise creditable film. Was it perhaps an acute sense that Jason resembled Eugene himself that contributed to Quintero's and Mann's decision to give him the role of Hickey? If so, the decision certainly worked.

That Hickey was based on O'Neill's brother Jamie is pretty generally agreed on. O'Neill's description of Hickey (quoted above) suggests a clear resemblance to Jamie O'Neill (see photographs in the

Sheaffer and Gelb biographies).[4] Hickey's raucous alcoholism and his being the much sought-after life of the party also resemble Jamie, as do his relationships with prostitutes (Hickey had to hide from his wife that he had contracted a venereal disease and Jamie having been a known womanizer). And finally Hickey's guilt is like Jamie's in being so all-out and so unself-forgiving.

The biographies tell us that the young Eugene emulated and idealized his older brother, especially Jamie's drinking and womanizing, and his general cynicism about life. Then, in the early 1920s, after Jamie's conduct following Ella O'Neill's death, so penetratingly treated in *A Moon for the Misbegotten*, Eugene turned against his brother, and refused to visit him during Jamie's dying days.[5] But that he continued to be deeply affected by Jamie is suggested by the fact that as early as 1920, he indicated he planned to write a "long play ... showing influence of elder on younger brother."[6] Shortly thereafter, he wrote *The Great God Brown*, in which the figures Billy Brown and Dion Anthony bear marked resemblances to the O'Neill brothers.

Throughout the 1930s and 1940s, O'Neill included several figures resembling Jamie in his plays. Such characters include Uncle Sid in *Ah, Wilderness!*, Loving (the hero's alter ego) in *Days Without End*, Hickey in *Iceman*, and Erie Smith in *Hughie*. He also, of course, included the literal Jamie in *Long Day's Journey* and *Misbegotten* as devastatingly cynical yet at the same time broadly generous figures struggling with gross moral deficiencies. As much as mother and father, his older brother was constantly on Eugene's mind as he wrote his late plays. The playwright was, in a way, still emulating him, now seeking his forgiveness.

Which brings us back to Jason's Hickey. First and most important of all, Jason resembled Eugene, not Jamie. Like Eugene, he was introspective, ectomorphic, and nervous. Quintero and Mann may have instinctively recognized Jason would play Hickey as essentially an introvert playing the role of an extrovert, which he did. Jason was Eugene pretending to be Jamie. Jason's Hickey was as original as it was because it caught the essential aspects of Jamie's personality with the essential aspects of Eugene's underlying it. The bluff, welcoming, hail-fellow-well-met was always there in Jason's interpretation, as was the ribald, barroom cynicism, and the salesman's proselytizing manner, which made Hickey the prototype of such later figures as Meredith

Willson's Professor Harold Hill. But equally characteristic of Jason in the role was the hard-edged nervousness, the tension underneath that threatened to break out at any moment. This combination was what made Jason's recital of Hickey's great confession in the last act so telling. Jason never ceased to be the salesman during the speech, even while he was revealing his desperate guilt. His nervous finger-snapping, for example, captured both the snake-oil hawker and the guilt-ridden self-tormentor at the same time.

Quintero continued seeing Jason in these terms when he cast Jason as Jamie in *Long Day's Journey* and *A Moon for the Misbegotten*. And Jason in those productions has almost obliterated any other image of Jamie. (Gabriel Byrne, who successfully played the role in the New York production of *Misbegotten* in spring 2000, was for me still in the Jason mold.) Again we had the introvert playing the extrovert, the balance between the two marvelously realized in *Misbegotten* by the delightful humor of the Jim Tyrone (i.e., Jamie)–Phil Hogan repartee set against Jason's rendition of the great confession of that play, which Jason made one of the most painful and most cathartic confessional arias of 20th-century theatre. And in spite of the fact that Edmund represents the younger Eugene in *Long Day's Journey*, it is again Jason's playing the role of Jamie as a wiser, forgiving O'Neill acting out his brother's *agon* that distinguishes Jason's treatment of the role. Jason's emphasis on Jamie's strength in the confrontation between the brothers during the last act, especially in the Sidney Lumet film version (which I remember best), gave audiences a sense of the tragic dimension O'Neill intended for Jamie Tyrone.

Jason Robards had the rare distinction of creating characterizations of the playwright himself playing the several personae of O'Neill's brother Jamie in O'Neill's later plays. In doing so Jason contributed mightily not only to O'Neill's theatrical legacy but also to our sense of one of the most deeply affecting aspects of O'Neill's biography, his struggle to come to terms with his brother's death.

NOTES

1. "Notable American Stage Productions," in *The Cambridge Companion to Eugene O'Neill*, ed. Michael Manheim (Cambridge, England: Cambridge University Press, 1998), 110.

2. At the meeting of the Eugene O'Neill Society held in Bermuda in January 1999, Ted Mann recalled that the intensity of Jason's tryout for the role and his determination to get it deeply affected his and Quintero's decision to cast him as Hickey.

3. For the full story of that production, see Gary Vena, O'Neill's "The Iceman Cometh": Reconstructing the Premiere (Ann Arbor, Mich.: UMI Research Press, 1998).

4. The only successful Jamie I have seen who looked a little like the real Jamie was Dennis Quilley, who played the role in the television version of the monumental Olivier production of Long Day's Journey Into Night in the early 1970s.

5. Most recently, Stephen A. Black's Eugene O'Neill: Beyond Mourning and Tragedy (New Haven: Yale University Press, 2000) explores the complex psychology underlying their relationship, and especially Eugene's difficulties in coming to terms with Jamie's death.

6. See Virginia Floyd, Eugene O'Neill at Work (New York: Frederick Ungar, 1981), 32. Floyd notes that O'Neill drew a faint line through that phrase, suggesting the abiding ambivalence in the playwright's feelings about his brother.

Not for Profit

by Sheila Hickey Garvey

> Sheila Hickey Garvey teaches theater at Southern Connecticut
> State University in New Haven and is President of the Eugene
> O'Neill Society, 2002–2003. The following are revised selec-
> tions excerpted from her book manuscript, "Not for Profit: A
> History of the Circle in the Square."

During rehearsals for the 1956 Circle in the Square revival of *The
Iceman Cometh*, the production's director, José Quintero, suffered no
restrictions on his artistic aims. But, partly out of a desire not to offend
Mrs. O'Neill and partly out of reverence for the eminent playwright's
work, Quintero carefully attempted to find a cast which would closely
resemble the precise physical descriptions of the characters which
O'Neill meticulously noted in the play. To do this, Quintero interviewed many actors and actresses and cast a number of actors such as
Farrell Pelly as Harry Hope and Peter Falk (at that time an unknown
actor) as Rocky the Bartender, without bothering to have them read.
They seemed to be the right "types" for the parts. Patricia Brooks, the
wife of José's partner Theodore Mann, who had also acted for Quintero in *The Grass Harp*, was ideal for the role of the feisty Pearl. Other
old friends in the cast included actress Gloria Scott Backe in the part
of Margie. She was then married to actor James Greene, who would
be playing the part of Jimmy Tomorrow.

Stage and screen character actor Howard da Silva was cast in the difficult role of Hickey, the play's central character. Having da Silva in the cast was a plus as he was a name actor who also had the stature and experience to carry the production. It was a terrible disappointment when da Silva dropped out of the production just before rehearsals began to take a better paying job: the Off Broadway minimum was the Circle's maximum, $30 a week. On the eve of beginning rehearsals Quintero was still searching for the right actor for Hickey, one who looked, according to O'Neill, "about fifty, a little under medium height, with a stout, roly-poly figure."[1] The right actor would also have to be willing to play the demanding role for meager wages. In the midst of the crisis, Jason Robards, Jr., who had appeared in the Circle's production of *American Gothic*, turned up at Quintero's office to request an audition. Robards had heard from his friend Jimmy Greene that Quintero was casting *The Iceman Cometh*.

When Greene was "between theatrical engagements" he could be found selling newspapers in a Greenwich Village corner stand. To give Greene business, Robards who lived in a nearby apartment with his wife Eleanore and their two children, would stop to buy a paper and talk about the theatre.[2] One morning Robards arrived at the stand to chat with Greene about the woes of being unemployed actors. Instead, he found Greene in a jovial mood. Jimmy and his wife Gloria were going to be in Quintero's latest production at the Circle in the Square, a revival of O'Neill's *Iceman*.

Robards began to sweat while asking Greene, "Is José still casting?" Greene's positive response set Robards running towards Sheridan Square. As he sprinted, he felt a simultaneous sense of panic and excitement. His thoughts raced, "I must be in that play... I've got to play Hickey."[3] In his mind he pictured the 1946 production with James Barton. While still a student at the American Academy, Robards had been taken for free to see the play and had been so fascinated by the work that he had paid to return and see Barton's replacement, E. G. Marshall. But Robards hadn't realized how deeply he had identified with the role of Hickey until his friend Jimmy told him about the upcoming Circle in the Square production.[4]

It was easy for Robards to get in to see Quintero. His work in *American Gothic* at the Circle in the Square two years before had been well-reviewed and during that production Jason and José had established an excellent rapport. As he rushed over to the Circle in the Square, Jason recalled that first audition for José. He had sung "The Summer Song," a tune Walter Huston had made famous in the movie *The Treasure of Sierra Madre*. José had complimented Jason on his audition, adding that he also liked his voice. Once Jason arrived at the Circle in the Square for his *Iceman* audition, he asked José if casting was still open for the role of Hickey. Quintero listened sympathetically to Jason's request to audition for the part but had to tell the very vulnerable actor standing before him that he did not match the physical description of the character given by O'Neill in the text. Instead, José offered Robards the part of the worst drunk in the bar, Willy Oban. It would be an ideal part for Jason, a young lawyer fallen on liquor and hard times who also sings songs. It was a character O'Neill modeled after his older brother Jamie. Robards pleaded with Quintero, begging for a chance to prepare an audition for the role of Hickey. More out of pity than anything else, Quintero relented.[5]

Days later, as Ted Mann was crossing through the corridor of the Circle in the Square, he almost collided with Jason Robards, who was hurrying into the theatre's cabaret area.[6] Mann noted a distinct scent of alcohol as Robards greeted him and then disappeared around the corner. Ted mentioned running into Jason to José and noted that Robards was particularly intense and agitated. About an hour and a half later, Quintero returned from auditions visibly elated. He announced to Mann and the Circle in the Square's Board of Directors, who had gathered for a meeting, that he had found the actor to play Hickey. Describing Robards' audition, he told them that the actor had given an astonishing reading, one that "illuminated the decadence of that role." Robards had memorized Hickey's last act speech about the death of Evelyn. In the darkened quiet of the cabaret standing on the wooden floorboards of the old dance floor, Robards had begun Hickey's confession: "I've got to tell you! Your being the way you are now gets my goat! It's all wrong! It puts things in my mind—about myself."[7] As the actor had weaved the chilling story Hickey tells of murdering his wife, Quintero sat stunned. Robards' presentation had hit Quintero so powerfully that he was "almost out of breath by the time that [Robards] had finished."[8] Even if he didn't look the part, he *was* the part. Quintero was going to go with Robards. With this crucial part settled, rehearsals for *The Iceman Cometh* could begin.

Because the run-throughs of the production were lasting four-and-a-half hours, Ted Mann scheduled a special 2 P.M. matinee opening performance on May 18, 1956. The afternoon preview would allow the specially invited audience of critics to digest the scope of the play and make their newspapers' deadlines. Tension backstage was especially high for this performance because preview audiences had not been receptive. The production was being viewed as a joke by a faction of critics who considered O'Neill a has-been. As Robards sat at his dressing table readying himself for Act I, he spotted Leigh Connell's reflection in his make-up mirror. The Circle in the Square producer had an "opening night" gift for the actor, one he hoped would bring the young actor inspiration. It was a recently published copy of a new and posthumously published O'Neill play called *Long Day's Journey Into Night*. Robards expressed his appreciation for the gift to Connell, saying he had heard about it and was looking forward to reading it. As Robards placed the book alongside his make-up kit, José appeared at the dressing room door to give some last-minute notes. Jason could feel José's intensity, something the director was trying to hide from the actor by conveying to him a sense of warmth and confidence. But Robards knew that the pressure was also on for Quintero, Connell, and Mann. The Circle in the Square would certainly be finished financially if this production didn't hit—and big.[9] And Jason, in the part of Hickey, held the burden of the responsibility for the theatre's future.

In a thoughtful and clever move, Ted Mann arranged for a free luncheon to be served from the bar in the theatre to the audience and the critics. The luncheon had a communion-like effect, creating a shared supper amongst all of the inhabitants of the bar, including the audience and the critics. They were partaking in a free meal compliments of Harry Hope. As the common meal ended, Act I began. All the elements needed to realize the full impact of the play were in place.[10]

Because the opening was occurring in mid-afternoon, streaks of light filtered through the cabaret's boarded windows and bled onto the playing area. The audience could see the actors on stage before the opening of each act. As the afternoon progressed, the performance progressed through O'Neill's first three acts. It was late afternoon when the performers began to take their places just prior to the beginning of Act IV. While they quietly entered and attempted to slip unobtrusively into their places they could be seen in the fading afternoon light. Suddenly the audience rose to their feet to give the cast a standing ovation. Robards was sitting at his dressing room table putting shadow under his eyes and blue on his beard to make himself look dissipated. He felt panic when he heard the applause. Running down the corridor past the coatroom, Jason collided with Quintero who was standing at the top of the steps leading to the audience area. Over the uproar, Robards shouted, "What the hell has happened? Do they think it's the end?" "No, no," laughed Quintero, "it's a damn symphony."[11] The audience, made up predominately of critics, was acknowledging the rebirth of a masterpiece.

When the applause finally began to subside, Act IV began. Eventually it was Robards' turn to make his entrance. The tension in the room was thick with anticipation. After exchanging the preliminary dialogue with the other onstage actors, Robards took his place at Harry Hope's bar. Peter Falk, who was playing Rocky the bartender, leaned over to Robards and whispered, "Don't blow it now, Jason."[12] He didn't.

That evening after the reviews came out, as was his practice, Ted Mann stood and read the notices to the cast and crew. The crucial review would come from *New York Times* critic Brooks Atkinson, who had found the 1946 Theatre Guild production of *Iceman* too long.[13] Mann read Atkinson's review to the cast first. Atkinson would lead a chorus of bravos when he said, "it seems not like something written, but like something that is happening."[14] In the *New York Herald Tribune*, Walter Kerr agreed with Atkinson and applauded Quintero's directorial approach which he described as "stunning patience." Kerr went on to compliment the acting company who "have examined and illuminated each successive, engraved-on-steel fragment."[15] The critical kudos were unanimous. The Circle in the Square had its first major success since *Summer and Smoke*. And just as that production had catapulted Geraldine Page to stardom, it was during his performance of Hickey in the Circle in the Square's production of *The Iceman Cometh* that Jason Robards gained lasting recognition as one of America's greatest actors.

While Robards was still performing downtown in *The Iceman Cometh*, he got the idea that the character of Willie Oban, the part Quintero had originally wanted him to play, was really an early version of the Jamie character he would soon be playing on Broadway in

José Quintero's upcoming production of *Long Day's Journey Into Night*. When Robards had some time offstage, he would watch Addison Powell's performance as Willie and look for traces of Jamie. Robards told Powell what he was doing and the two discussed the similarities.

In comparing Iceman to *Long Day's Journey*, Powell could see that "Willie had the emotional demands in it that Jamie has, the depth of his despair and self destruction ... you've got the father, that's cut from the same plot, and you've got the bitter humor. The self-destructive humor of Willie is very much like Jamie." After one performance, Robards and Powell talked and Robards admitted, "I'm going to be using Willie—not literally. It's just coming in on me strongly that that scene [*Iceman* Act I] has so many drum beats foreshadowing Jamie's big scene in *Long Day's Journey*."[16]

Once Robards left *Iceman* and was able to rehearse full-time with the rest of the *Long Day's Journey* cast, he began to identify with the character of Jamie Tyrone. It was probably time for him to leave *Iceman* anyway. The depressing and cruel aspects of the play were starting to affect him in strange ways. He was an actor who sought realism and truth in his performances, something he had learned from one of his favorite teachers at the American Academy, Charles Jehlinger. Yet the dark and disturbing, almost evil, nature of the play was causing Robards to push against the boundaries of life and art. During one performance and in the final act when Hickey confesses his hatred for Evelyn's repeated forgiveness of his negligence, he had said "Eleanore" instead of Evelyn. Eleanore was his wife's name. They were having marital problems but Jason didn't want to confuse his life and his work. His own father was an actor, and Jason had seen first hand that actors could have difficult personal lives. But, clearly, *Iceman* had begun to place a strain on Jason's complicated personal life and also on his subconscious mind.[17]

Starting rehearsals full-time for *Long Day's Journey Into Night*, however, only took him out of one crucible and placed him in another. The character of Jamie Tyrone had the same kind of life parallels in it for Jason that Hickey did but even more so. There was the distant relationship between Jamie and his mother. Theirs is a conflicted love/hate relationship which Jamie blames on her abandonment of him to boarding schools and eventually to drug addiction. Robards could easily relate to Jamie's anger at his mother. When studying the script, something he did almost compulsively, he was fascinated to discover that his character spoke directly to his mother only once during the entire four-hour play.[18] Robards understood Jamie's need to reject his mother by indirectly ignoring her. His own parents had divorced when he was only five years old. Because his father was an actor and was often away on tour, he and his brother had been sent away to boarding schools at too young and too vulnerable an age. His relationship to his mother was further strained when she "remarried, and resigned her children's care to their father."[19] She barely participated in their life after that.

There were other breathtaking parallels between Robards' life and feelings and those of Jamie Tyrone. Like the elder James Tyrone, Robards' father had been a highly regarded stage actor. Like Tyrone and Jamie, both Robards Sr. and Jr. drank too much. And, like Jamie, Robards loved his father but considered him an actor who had sold out. Like Tyrone, Robards' father was a "matinee idol," an extremely handsome and charming man, compelling to women. Tyrone was a nineteenth-century classical actor who had turned to playing melodramas, in particular *The Count of Monte Cristo*, to make money. Robards Sr. had a promising stage career in New York but had spent the major portion of his career playing character parts in Hollywood movies in the 1930s and 1940s. Jason Jr. had endured his father's personal and professional failures with fear and bitterness. When his only available parent suffered, Jason suffered.

During one of many newspaper interviews for the production, Robards Jr. spoke in a stream of consciousness conversation with Arthur Gelb about parallels between his life and Jamie's. Fully aware that he was speaking to a newspaperman, Robards still found himself confessing, "When I was little, my father was one of the biggest names in Hollywood. Suddenly—and how it happened to him was always a great mystery to me—he wasn't a star anymore; he was on the fringe. From the time I was fourteen, I was always conscious of a sense of worry, of terrific insecurity—agents, phony talk, the waits for the phone to ring. It's not what I considered living."[20] Repulsed by his father's repeated anxieties, Jason spurned acting as a career and joined the Navy to find escape and structure. He was assigned to Pearl Harbor and was stationed there on December 7th, 1941. His seven years in the Navy taught him what he needed to know. After the War ended,

Robards Jr. decided that a life of safety was impossible for him. He would become an actor. He decided to train at his father's old school, the American Academy of Dramatic Arts. After graduation, Jason began to pursue his acting career in New York.

Performing in O'Neill's *Iceman* and *Long Day's Journey* were achievements beyond his wildest dreams, more than his father had achieved in his own career. Jason used all of the angst he felt about his upbringing and put it into his acting work. It was the only way Robards Jr. knew to purge his own personal demons. During performances of *Long Day's Journey Into Night,* Jason even began to think that Fredric March looked like his own father. For Jason Robards Jr., being in *Long Day's Journey Into Night* was like walking into a theater to perform his own life.[21]

Long Day's Journey Into Night closed March 29, 1958, after a run of sixty-five weeks and 389 performances. Fredric March (James Tyrone) had always had the habit of peeking out at the audience before the curtain's rise to check the house. One night near the end of the run, March looked out and could see that the house was "thin." Turning to the other actors waiting to make their entrances backstage, he quipped, "there must be a big dance in Newark tonight."[22] March and his wife, the actress Florence Eldridge (Mary Tyrone), had been asked to do the upcoming London production. But by the time the show was ready to close in New York they were tired. The play was brutal to perform. The amount of energy that it took to give each performance would have taxed a young football player. But what was more important to them in making their decision was that Jason Robards Jr. and Brad Dillman had long since left the show to pursue movie careers. The original company had become like a family. One particularly touching incident moved them all. Jason Robards Jr. had invited his father Jason Robards Sr. to have a special seat set up for him backstage where the senior Robards could watch a performance of the play like a dignitary and a member of the production company. The elder Robards and March were old friends and the presence of Jason Jr.'s actor/father backstage gave a sense of meaning to the performance of the play that only theatre people, whose lives are irrevocably entwined with the arts, could really understand. That night, Jason Jr. was so tender and attentive to his father during offstage moments that the entire company noted their relationship. They witnessed a doting son hovering about his father, even sitting at his feet while whispering affectionately to him in hushed comforting tones.

It was not the only personal situation that Robards had brought directly into the production. Ted Mann had unexpectedly ended up babysitting Jason's children late one afternoon. This occurred during a marital crisis, a problem so severe it couldn't be hidden. Robards asked Ted if he would take care of his children while he ran to the theater to get ready for the evening performance. Robards' wife Eleanore was too emotionally ill to handle the children. In an effort to help out both Robards and the production, Mann had dutifully rushed over to the couple's apartment. Returning to the theater well into the performance, Mann experienced, firsthand, the way Jason could use his personal pain to inform his acting work. Mann would later recall watching Jason during the Act IV scene between Jamie and Edmund during which Jamie spews with vitriolic abandon, "you've got to tie a can to me—get me out of your life—think of me as dead—tell people, 'I had a brother but he's dead.' And when you come back, look out for me. I'll be waiting to welcome you with that 'my old pal stuff' and give you the glad hand, and at the first good chance I get stab you in the back."[23] Mann would later recall that it was then that he really came to understand Jason's work as an actor. Ted saw a rage in Jason on stage that was terrifying and real. Mann would remember that particular performance of Jason's as being the best one the actor gave during the production's entire run.

Such incidents made the company of *Long Day's Journey Into Night* more than a superior acting company, it made them a family. But after Robards and Dillman had left the original company, the chemistry in the performances was different, still good, but different. Having reaped many rewards from the acclaimed production, the Marches decided to forgo another strenuous run of the play and opted out of the planned London production.

For professional and personal reasons, José Quintero and Jason Robards ended their contracts with the Lincoln Center Repertory Company in 1964. Since both Quintero and Robards were "between engagements" they decided to try to mount an often contemplated project. It would be the American premiere of O'Neill's one-act, *Hughie*. It was a project they had been planning to do since 1958 when Quintero had first thought of staging it at the Spoleto Festival. At that time Mrs. O'Neill had instead decided to give the premiere rights to produce *Hughie* to Stockholm's Royal Dramatic Theatre which had also presented the world premiere of *Long Day's Journey Into Night*. Mrs. O'Neill had promised Theodore Mann and José Quintero the rights to produce *Hughie* immediately after its opening in Stockholm but that production never materialized because other projects interfered. A recent and successful London production of *Hughie* starring Burgess Meredith in the role of Erie and Jack MacGowran as the Night Clerk had prompted Quintero to reconsider mounting the project. Since the rights were jointly held by Mann and Quintero, José asked his now former partner Ted Mann if he would consider co-producing the piece.[24] Once Mann had agreed, Quintero invited producer Joseph E. Levine, who had produced the film version of *Long Day's Journey Into Night*, to be a co-producer in association with Gabriel Kathzka and Gustave Berne. Shortly thereafter, David Hays agreed to be the production's set and lighting designer. The production team seemed one likely to be responsible for creating another O'Neill theatrical landmark. Robards was given the standard six-month run-of-the-play contract with an option to renew in June of 1965.

Hughie was the only surviving one-act play from a series O'Neill had been writing titled "By Way of Obit." Written in 1942, *Hughie* had been one of the last of O'Neill's writings which he had allowed Carlotta to preserve for posterity after his death. Although the play was an intimate two-character, one-hour piece, it had potential as a project of significance and stature on the American stage. The decision was made to mount the show at Broadway's Royale Theatre rather than in a smaller Off Broadway house in anticipation of strong audience interest.

Robards had already been working on the piece, and found it excellent actor-based material and a complex exercise in self-discipline. The major difficulty for the actor playing the part of Erie was that so much of the burden for sustaining the plot falls on one character, the one Robards would play. Like Hickey's lengthy monologue, which Robards had mastered when playing in *The Iceman Cometh*, Erie's long monologues were a fascinating acting challenge. Erie Smith was like the role of Hickey in *The Iceman Cometh* in that it was the kind of part that would take even an accomplished actor years to master.

A special kind of actor was also needed to play the role of the Night Clerk. The seemingly empty character had to be performed by a top-notch support player. Both Quintero and Robards agreed that Jack Dodson, an actor who had worked frequently under Quintero at the Circle in the Square, best fit the job and the part.

Although Quintero and Robards had made considerable efforts to find a companion piece to play as a "second act" or "curtain opener" to *Hughie,* they had come to the conclusion that, although short, the piece was powerful and would be able to sustain an evening on its own. The decision to let the piece stand by itself was risky and not well-received.

The critical responses to the December 22, 1964, opening were mixed. Norman Nadel of the *New York World-Telegram and Sun* credited Robards' performance as Erie with having "enormous virtuosity" and praised Jack Dodson's Night Clerk for conveying "eloquent emptiness" but fault was found with various aspects of the production.[25] In particular, he questioned the decision made to stage the play at the Royale Theatre. In the *New York Post* Richard Watts Jr. wrote that "The Royale stage seems rather to overwhelm so intimate a play."[26] Howard Taubman's *New York Times* review concurred, citing the "uncommon width of the stage" as dwarfing what he believed was a play that was a mere "sketching in small what [O'Neill] drew grandly elsewhere."[27]

After it closed on Broadway on January 30, 1965, *Hughie* began a profitable road tour, opening first at Los Angeles' Huntington Hartford Theatre before moving on to San Francisco's Curran Theatre. The production was met with more favorable reviews than it had received in New York. The play fared better on the road notably due to the presence of Jason Robards Jr. in its cast. Robards, now a highly acclaimed stage and film actor, was a star that West Coast audiences had never been able to see before in person.

Although *Hughie*'s American premiere did not launch the play on a straight path to glory, it would eventually become one of Robards' primary acting vehicles. Robards knew that, despite the critics' negative opinions, his rendition of Erie Smith, as directed by José Quintero, was one of the best and most important roles available to him in the O'Neill repertoire. In the years to come and throughout his career, Erie Smith would be a character Robards would revisit and deepen.

These performances would always occur under the guidance and direction of José Quintero.

In 1964, because of their association with the Circle in the Square, Robards, Quintero and the plays of Eugene O'Neill were only beginning what would become a long life's journey. It was a destiny with a grandeur and meaning they could not possibly envision during those early and formative years.

NOTES

1. Eugene O'Neill, *The Iceman Cometh* (New York: Random House, 1946), 76.

2. Personal interview with James Greene, The John F. Kennedy Center for the Performing Arts, Washington D.C. 12 Aug. 1985.

3. Personal interview with Jason Robards, The John F. Kennedy Center for the Performing Arts, Washington D.C. 12 Aug. 1985.

4. Interview, Robards, 1985.

5. Archives the Circle in the Square, Interview of Mann for Channel 13 television.

6. Interview, Mann.

7. Eugene O'Neill. *The Plays of Eugene O'Neill* (New York: Random House, 1954), 708.

8. "Eugene O'Neill: The Later Years" conference, Suffolk University, Boston, 31 May 1986.

9. Interview, Greene.

10. Interview, Greene.

11. Howard Greenberger, *The Off-Broadway Experience* (Englewood Cliffs, N.J.: Prentice-Hall, 1971) 46, 47.

12. Interview, Robards, 1985.

13. Brooks Atkinson, "Theatre: O'Neill Tragedy Revived," *New York Times*, 9 May 1956.

14. Walter Kerr, "Little Hope of Hope," *New York Times*, 9 May 1956.

15. Kerr.

16. Edwin J. McDonough, *Quintero Directs O'Neill* (Chicago: A Cappella Books, 1991), 57–59.

17. Barbara Gelb, "Jason Jamie Robards Tyrone," *New York Times Magazine*, 20 Jan. 1974, 64.

18. B. Gelb.

19. B. Gelb

20. Arthur Gelb, "Long Journey Into Light," *New York Times*, 25 Nov. 1956.

21. Interview, Jason Robards, 10 Nov. 1998.

22. Interview, Theodore Mann, The Circle in the Square Theatre, 6 June 1986.

23. Eugene O'Neill, *Long Day's Journey Into Night* (New Haven: Yale University Press, 1955), 166.

24. Interview, Robards, 1985.

25. Norman Nadel, "O'Neill's 'Hughie' Is Too Limited," *The New York World-Telegram and The Sun*, 23 Dec. 1964.

26. Richard Watts, Jr. "A Late O'Neill Character Study," *New York Post* 23 Dec. 1964.

27. Howard Taubman, "Robards and Dodson in American Premiere," *New York Times*, 23 Dec. 1964.

On Jason Robards as O'Neill's Nietzschean Iceman

by Stephen A. Black

Stephen A. Black's most recent book is the biography *Eugene O'Neill: Beyond Mourning and Tragedy* (Yale University Press, 1999). The essay below first appeared in *The Eugene O'Neill Review*, vol. 17, 1 & 2, Spring/Fall 1993, pp. 149–56, and is reprinted with the kind permission of the editor of the *Review*, Frederick Wilkins.

The Iceman Cometh makes extreme demands on anyone who approaches it, no less on its audiences than on its performers. I write, from the point of view of a spectator, about a 1960 television performance of the play, featuring the actor most identified with major roles in the later O'Neill plays, Jason Robards. Mr. Robards' performance as Hickey, the salesman, in a production directed by Sidney Lumet, enlarges the meaning of the play to its audience, and helps the audience meet the play's demands. I will not say that the 1960 performance makes the play coherent because its author did that; but the performance helps the audience feel the play's coherence.

Performances of *Iceman* may not always seem whole and integral to an audience, and I need to speak briefly about certain problems before proceeding to my main subject. The problems revolve around

40

two difficult theatrical and literary ideas, "realism" and "tragedy." What "tragedy" means to O'Neill we will come to shortly.

An audience may find much in *Iceman* that resembles ordinary life, but there is also much that one doesn't see every day. Travis Bogard once called the conversation in the bar "choric," correctly underscoring the play's musical structure. O'Neill himself, in a 1931 notebook entry, spoke of "my unconscious use of musical structure in nearly all of my plays ... using rhythm of recurrent themes" (qtd. in *Eugene O'Neill at Work*, ed. Virginia Floyd [New York: Ungar, 1981], 228–229). In *Iceman* a theme is carried by one voice, then passes on to another that changes the key and figure before yielding to someone else who makes further changes. Think of Berlioz or Mahler or Shostakovich. For a moment, think of the bums, not as individuals who speak English, but as orchestral sounds. Imagine Jimmy Tomorrow as viola, Larry as first violin, Rocky as second violin, Oban as trumpet, Hope as cello, Mosher and McGloin as tuba and bassoon, Parritt as oboe, Hickey as horn—and so on. Larry is the leader of a chorus that sometimes speaks or acts in unison. Once noticed, the play's musical structure is obvious.

It is less obvious that O'Neill splits the central tragic figure into two characters—Hickey and the boy Parritt. They are "members of the same lodge," both maddened by guilt, and both doomed to die in ritualistic acts of self-sacrifice. We know they are one because from time to time they actually merge. They speak each other's unspoken thoughts, and answer remarks the other has thought but not yet said.

Splitting the central tragic figure between two actors takes the play out of the realm of realism, in which an individual actor impersonates another individual. What is evoked through the impersonations of Hickey and Parritt is the spirit of a figure we dimly sense lingering in the mythic background of the play. One way O'Neill makes *Iceman* coherent is by elaborating the myth at the center of Nietzsche's notion of the tragic. (The following quotations from Nietzsche may be found in Section 10 of *The Birth of Tragedy*. The passages quoted are identical in the translations read by O'Neill and attributed to Thomas Commons [published about 1925 by The Modern Library], and that by Walter Kaufmann [Vintage, 1967], 73–76.)

The myth relates the ritual sufferings of Dionysus, which Nietzsche said was the "sole theme" of Greek tragedy. In this myth, as Nietzsche retells it, the god takes on human form, suffers, dies, and is transformed. But because the god is not mortal, the community gains consolation from his death. In consolation, the god gives mortals the grape. Beyond ease of pain, the death of a god infuses regenerative power "into air, water, earth and fire." The god's human body is torn to pieces and its blood and flesh ploughed into the soil. The earth heals and renews itself and life goes on even if human individuals do not.

Individuation implies the death of the individual, and from dread of death comes the alienation of people from nature. But tragic art gives us "the joyous hope that the spell of individuation may be broken in augury of a restored oneness." Thus Nietzsche links the ancient mystery to the consequence of its loss in the modern world, the alienation that defines his time and ours.

With Nietzsche in mind, we may think of *The Iceman Cometh* as a play without realistic characters. Hickey and Parritt are parts of a shadow-figure we may call Dionysus, but may never see directly. All the actors have many lines, yet there is no character development of the sort that O'Neill gives—say—Josie Hogan in *A Moon for the Misbegotten*. The bums talk about the past, but only to justify asking others to accept their pipe dreams. They are mythical members of a mythical society that works like any human society, and the pipe dreams represent the protection society gives people from knowledge of individuation and death. It's a mutual back-scratching society and, as Act One shows, most of the time it works pretty well. The first act, as O'Neill once acknowledged, is comic.

Parritt is an intruder into the back-scratching society, so nakedly alienated that his mere presence reminds the bums how little separates them from the knowledge they can't bear. Most of the time they can ignore their mortality. But when knowledge of death intrudes, it brings awareness that mortal knowledge has never been farther away than the next drink or the next reassurance that someone else believes one's pipe dream. And so they hate Parritt on sight, and shun him. Parritt carries openly what Hickey has always concealed.

Mentioning Hickey's alienation brings me to my main subject: to try to say what Jason Robards does, in that 1960 television performance, that allows us to understand the play in another context than realism. I thank Mr. Sydney Lumet for permitting me to use a video tape of the performance for study purposes.

From the moment we first lay eyes on Robards' Hickey, near the end of Act One, we are made to know how different a world he inhabits from that of the bums, or from that of life outside the theatre—or even life in the D.T. ward at Bellevue. In a rare close up—the film is shot mostly at middle distances—we see Hickey's face almost filling the screen, his pale, grinning mug framed by the wide round brim of his light straw hat which is pushed as far back as it will go. The hat brim looks like a disc and frames a gaunt face. The image seems not quite three-dimensional, and the grin on the face is half-clownish, half-spectral; it's an abstract design of a mask as much as it is a realistic image of a face. Hickey's suit is neat and dark; his cuffs, his collar and the flower in his lapel are sparkling white; and his face is nearly as pale as his linen. His cuffs stick out of his coat sleeves at least four inches, emphasizing the contrast between light and dark. A few minutes later, when he has begun his salvation spiel and assures his friends, "nothing up my sleeve, honest," Robards has Hickey pull his coat sleeves to his elbows. His paleness, the black and white costume, and the exaggerated, mugging grin continue to suggest something of the clown, and remind us why the bums long for Hickey's visits: because he can always make them laugh and forget the blues.

Hickey reminds the audience of Pedrolino, Pierrot, the moon-faced, the martyr. But on this visit to the bar he is not the sort of clown one laughs at. To Larry he is the iceman of death. The other bums also sense that he is more remote than usual from their world. They have always seen Hickey as one of them, just one still living the pipe dream that the others have consigned to past and future. The play shows him gradually becoming aware of his alienation. He cannot enjoy the society of Hope's bar, but has come to announce a better consolation than booze and pipe dreams.

Robards' performance is so complex that we can never imagine we understand everything going on. Even at the beginning there are many questions we cannot answer. When Hickey notices Parritt, the stage directions tell us he feels puzzled; he senses some recognition he can't grasp but says he knows they are "members of the same lodge." To escape the confusion that recognizing Parritt creates in him, Hickey squabbles with Larry and seems hurt when Larry tells him to mind his own business. As always when he is shaken, Hickey tries to return to his clown's role; he urges everyone to drink up and apologizes for being a pain in the neck. When Larry challenges him on the salvation he's selling, Hickey deflects the challenge, but he moves away from Larry. He tries to recover his heartiness with a joke: "What is this, a funeral?" It's the wrong joke and no one laughs. He orders them to drink up, and they do—but without joy.

Hickey stumbles over a chair and is saved from falling by Joe, who picks up the chair. A two-beat pause, during which we see only Hickey's rigid back, makes it plain that the little jolt has deeply shaken the salesman. He steps forward again but runs into the corner of Joe's table and doubles over in pain. He now turns around toward the camera, his back to the bums. His face is ghastly, as if he has glimpsed the Nietzschean void. O'Neill tells us he yawns and his voice becomes muffled with drowsiness. He sits down and begins apologizing for going "dead on you like this." Thoughts of pipe dreams make him instantly drowsy, and from morphia his mind drifts to the loss of his last pipe dream and to sinking to the bottom of the sea.

Perhaps no real salesman can permit himself to have a crisis of philosophical skepticism, but that is exactly what Robards here shows Hickey doing. If we don't get all that the actor is doing, at least we are jogged away from believing that what we see is the ordinary. We may begin to notice the difference between stage realism and the world that skeptical philosophy has in mind when it claims that philosophy cannot prove the existence of knowledge about the world.

The Iceman Cometh transforms the paradoxes of philosophical skepticism into experience of the most immediate kind. By a thousand details in the text, O'Neill leads his iceman away from commonsense reality. Robards follows O'Neill to that world described by Nietzsche where the "sole theme" of tragedy is "the suffering of Dionysus," where all the "celebrated figures of the Greek stage—Prometheus, Oedipus, etc.—are mere masks of ... Dionysus," where "behind all these masks there is a deity...." Belief in the reality of death and belief in the world's renewal are some of O'Neill's answers to the problem of skepticism. In a strange way, knowing that we are mortal helps us tolerate knowing that no other knowledge we have is necessarily reliable. Robards makes himself the vehicle for the expression of O'Neill's strange, paradoxical optimism.

Behind one of the masks of Dionysus, Robards embodies the god-as-man disintegrating in a psychic sparagmos, a dismemberment of the soul. Dismemberment of the god, Nietzsche believed, symbolized liberating the god's spirit from its fleshly confinement to return to the elements, earth, fire and water, as required for the mystery of regeneration. Hickey is dismembered by humiliation and rejection. O'Neill emphasizes renewing the community's soul over the renewal of the earth's body. Expressing such an idea, dramatically, is what O'Neill requires; and it is what Robards gives us.

Robards' performance teaches us the difference between mythic and psychiatric thinking. There are a number of realistic ways that Hickey may be played. First, he may be played as a near-psychopath, whose destructive life takes him from the murder of his wife, to disrupting the fellowship in the bar, to a future in which, we may speculate, he will play out the same action in a law court and then in an asylum that he has played in the bar. Or Hickey may be played as simply the happy-go-lucky slob he says he is, who can't untangle the complications of his life and in a moment of extremity tries to solve all the problems with a single desperate act. Or he may be played as a man who has always hovered near psychosis; unable to tolerate guilt or anxiety and devoted to a wife who makes him feel both guilty and anxious, he murders her in a fit of agitated depression, after which his mood changes to a benevolent, manic high which shields him from understanding the reality of the act and from feeling any remorse. In his state of mind he does not believe she is really dead; the boundary between living and dying has vanished, and the murder has not really happened. With motives only partly glimpsed, and in a demonstrably calculating way, he sets out to create for his friends the conditions that will make them feel as awful as Evelyn had made him feel by her indomitable goodness and forgiveness. In all these realistic readings, Hickey goes to the bar to persuade his friends to assure him that the only thing he could have done, for Evelyn's sake, was to kill the poor woman.

Robards does not play Hickey in ways that exclude such realistic interpretations, but neither does he restrict our understanding to the ordinary. He gives us something more, something that entitles us to think of the play in the way we think about the greatest Greek tragedies. By the complexity of his performance Robards turns Hickey into a sacred fool and sacrificial goat, who gathers into himself the guilt, anxieties, follies and desperation of his fellows. He offers his own humiliation and alienation to expunge for a while the community's dread of dying and its collective self-hatred. Hickey the realistic character has no such intent; not exactly. But playwright and actor conspire to offer, simultaneously, a Hickey who goes beyond what the man might be, who becomes a sop to the bloodthirsty earth-gods of the goat-song.

By the tricks of costume, mime and mugging in Act One, Robards signals the audience to be alert. They are signs that things will not be simple or straightforward. Most of what he does is infinitely subtle, and so swift and complex as to defy analysis while it's happening.

From the moment of his entrance in Act Four, Robards launches at the audience and the bums a cascade of shifts and changes: of moods, thoughts, emotional tricks and challenges. His vocal tones carry meanings different from the substance of his words, and his face often suggests still different feelings and thoughts. The changes are so complex, and come so quickly and often, that we can hardly try to keep up with them, let alone understand them all as they occur. I originally intended to try to describe verbally all the shifts and changes in a brief passage; but I found, after studying the videotape of the Lumet film, that having played a two- or three-minute-long sequence over and over, making notes as well as I could, I still knew I had missed a great deal. I found I must settle for catching and conveying only some of it. The effect of the cascade of changes is a flood of emotional demands pushing and pulling audience and bums in all directions. By the changes the actor responds to the complex demands of the text, using O'Neill's stage directions as hints to what the character feels. Robards has found ways to know the feelings, and he is the actor to express them. The enormous compression of so many simultaneous states of mind shows Hickey feeling and thinking everything the others experience, metaphysical or ordinary.

In Act Four Hickey enters just as Larry tells Rocky that the salesman will be back because he's beginning to wonder if the peace he has sold is "the real McCoy." Perhaps Hickey has been poised at the door, listening to what the bums say about him before he enters. Then, indignantly, angrily, and with a little clear desperation, Hickey gives the lie. But his wrinkled clothes and weary face show he's lost his previous euphoria. He tries to hide his anger at Larry by pretending that the outburst was kidding, but he shows his confusion. No one will look

at him, and Rocky shuns him. Hickey tries to regain his command-
ing, benevolent tone, but when Hope complains that he has done something to the booze, Hickey loses his temper again. "Are you still harping
on that damned nonsense?" He whines, then shifts mechanically back
to his spiel and excuses his irritation. In another moment he changes
again, sounding honestly bewildered: he wonders why the others aren't
peaceful and contented, as if he had forgotten what he had previously
known—how much his assaults hurt them. Then he changes again. "I
know from my own experience," he insists, his voice childlike: "But
I've explained that a million times!" His voice becomes almost wist-
ful: "By rights you should be contented now without a single damned
lying pipe dream left to torment you." In an instant his face is con-
torted with pain and confusion; but the words he speaks seem meant
as a wisecrack: "Here you are, acting like a lot of stiffs cheating the
undertaker." If it is a joke, nobody laughs because his voice and face
reflect such a multitude of cacophonous thoughts.

O'Neill has Hickey "look around accusingly" at the others and
say: "I can't figure it—unless it's just your damned pigheaded stub-
bornness!" I recall another actor speaking this line with a threatening,
paranoid manner, as if Hickey is angry at the bums for making him
feel bad. It is a poor choice of readings for it risks allowing the audience to see Hickey as merely a psychiatric case. Robards speaks the
lines like a confused, hurt little boy. "Hell," he says, "you oughtn't to
act this way with me! You're the only pals I've got."

From here until his exit with the policemen, Robards shifts, with
voice and face, from seeming the phony-hearty salesman to seeming
a lost, lonely child. The rush of feelings overloads the audience. In a
single moment we may pity Hickey's pain, resent his spieling, hate his
cruelty, understand that he's spieling to try to keep from falling apart,
pity his disintegration, and be terrified at the glimpse he gives us of
what he sees in himself and in the world.

With another actor, the long narrative of Hickey's romance with
Evelyn and of the murder might seem only horrifying, and the salesman might seem increasingly alien and monstrous to people of conscience. But Robards makes the tale of confused love and murder
pitiable as well as terrible. He makes it difficult to watch and hear
Hickey's narrative without empathizing, against one's conscience, with
the terrible desperate act, and empathizing, against one's conscience,

with the suffering of the man who did it as well as with the woman who died. One disapproves and condemns; but with Robards as Hickey it is hard to doubt that he means it when he says, at the end, "Oh I want to go [to the chair], Officer. I can hardly wait now.... I've got to explain to Evelyn." Robards' Hickey has never known what death is, nor accepted its permanence. In this way and otherwise, Hickey and his alter-ego Parritt take into their collective self the qualities of all mortals, and stumble, half-willing, half blind, to the end we all dread and deny. However they have injured the fellowship in the bar, once they are gone, society can forgive and find consolation for what life does to everyone.

The Iceman Cometh may be the greatest of O'Neill's plays. It stands comfortably beside Oedipus at Colonus and Lear. It conceives a tragedy which captures the essential dread of our world. Yet, like Oedipus at Colonus, it wraps tragedy in a mantle of consolation and forgiving— the consolation of drunken singing and laughter. As realism, Hickey and his story may seem intolerable. But O'Neill and Robards conspire to make Hickey's madness less psychiatric than Dionysian.

Jason Robards helped us know how great a play The Iceman Cometh is.

Long Journey Into Light

by Arthur Gelb

Arthur Gelb was Cultural Editor and later Managing Editor of the *New York Times*. He is now President of the *New York Times* Foundation. He is co-author with Barbara Gelb of *O'Neill: Life with Monte Cristo* (Applause Books, 2000), volume 1 of a revised and expanded edition of a biography considered a standard work since 1962. The following article appeared in the *New York Times* on November 25, 1956. Copyright © 1956 by the New York Times Co. Reprinted by permission of the *Times* and the author.

Jason Robards Jr. wears the role of Jamie Tyrone, the older son in *Long Day's Journey Into Night*, like a second skin. For Robards feels himself to be closely attuned to the spirit of O'Neill and particularly to the character of the despairing Jamie, who represents O'Neill's elder brother in the autobiographical play.

The 34-year-old actor is, like Jamie, the son of a once famous matinee idol. (Robards Sr. was a star of the silent screen, by whom young Jason felt overshadowed). Like Jamie, who tries to drown his self-disappointment in drink, Robards was at one time inclined to look for a way out in alcohol. (Psychoanalysis helped him curb this tendency.) And finally, like O'Neill himself and a number of characters he has drawn, Robards knocked about at sea for many of his youthful years. (He was at Pearl Harbor when the Japanese attacked.)

The four Tyrones in the 1956 American premiere production of *Long Day's Journey Into Night*. Seated: Florence Eldridge (Mary), Fredric March (James); standing, Bradford Dillman (Edmund), Jason Robards Jr. (Jamie). Used by permission of the Billy Rose Theatre Collection, The New York Public Library for the Performing Arts, and the Astor, Lenox and Tilden Foundations.

The resemblance, happily, ends there. For O'Neill, with his superb flair for wringing from any reasonably maladjusted creature the last, bitter drop of tragedy, painted Jamie in bigger-than-life strokes of anguish and brutality. Robards is only life-size—six feet when he straightens out of his habitual slouch—and, while introverted and sensitive, with the O'Neillian tough veneer, he can scarcely be said to be plunging toward an O'Neillian doom. In fact, while shoving Jamie down the road to perdition every night, Robards himself is actually poised on the edge of success. He has been twice singled out in recent months for brilliant work in two O'Neill plays—first for his portrayal of Hickey in the Circle in the Square revival of *The Iceman Cometh* and currently, of course, for his violent and vivid impersonation of Jamie at the Helen Hayes.

Robards is a spare man with a long face that ends in a jutting chin. His deep-set, tired eyes and his dark hair flecked with gray make him look weathered beyond his years. His slouch, which he calls a baseball stoop, was acquired in the course of an intensely athletic youth, during which he often assumed a catcher's stance. He makes broad, fluent gestures with his hands and, when shyness makes him grope for a phrase, he sometimes snaps his fingers together nervously.

This gesturing of the hands and a dry, slightly self-conscious chuckle are mannerisms that do not leave him onstage; they were part of Hickey's character and are now a part of Jamie's, but in both cases they blend into painstakingly thoughtful and introspective characterizations—by virtue of acting techniques not, for a wonder, learned at the Actors Studio. Robards has never been near the Studio, as he happens to feel that television has given him an ideal training ground.

"I've been in 200 TV shows," said Robards the other day, over his third cup of coffee at Sardi's—where he had been only twice before: "I've played all kinds of TV roles, from cowboys to fathers of teenagers. It's helped me a lot. Of course, I was very lucky to have had good directors."

As for his stage work, in 1952 it was providing him with just about enough to starve on. He had come back from a year's road tour in *Stalag 17*. His wife and two young children had plodded after him from city to city (their 5-month-old Sarah slung from her mother's shoulder in an improvised canvas hammock and 3-year-old Jason sturdily making his own way).

A united family was about the sum total of Robards' assets when he hit New York. He could not find a job on Broadway. His television contacts (fairly tenuous at the time of his departure, anyway) had withered away. He took a $60-a-month cold water flat in the meat-packing district of Greenwich Village.

Eventually Robards landed a leading role in José Quintero's Circle in the Square production of *American Gothic*, which ran for seventy-seven performances in 1953. He was praised by the critics and within a few months of the closing, major television roles began flowing steadily his way.

When he heard last spring that Quintero was casting *Iceman*, he applied for the role of Hickey and got it after one reading. It was inevitable that Quintero should have picked him for his uptown production of *Journey*.

Notwithstanding this stepped-up professional activity, the Robards family continued to heat water over a gas stove in the Village so they could save to pay off an accumulation of debts. It is only now that the success of *Journey* seems assured that they are looking around for less Spartan quarters. They have also apportioned a good slice of the new budget to some square meals for the head of the family. No one ever tangled truly and well with O'Neill without showing some scars, and Robards has lost twenty of his normal 165 pounds since he started playing Hickey. In fact, he has to fake a bit in *Journey* where Fredric March, as Jamie's father, comments, "The hot sun will sweat some of that booze fat off you." This is Robards' cue to increase his slouch, push down his belt and thrust his stomach out in a brave attempt to simulate the non-existent booze fat.

In addition to weight loss, a feeling of exhaustion after each performance is the price Robards is paying for the privilege of doing two mammoth O'Neill roles without a break between. "When I do the long fourth-act drunk scene," he said, "my hands become covered with sweat and I get athlete's cotton mouth the way I did when I used to run cross-country at Hollywood High School."

Robards thinks the tension may be partly due to his close sense of identity with Jamie. "Jamie is the kind of drunk I understand. He uses drinking to be more drunk than he actually is—he's a two-purpose drunk—the kind who, when he really wants to say something, says it and then covers up as a drunk. He switches back and forth.

That's the way I used to drink during the seven years I was in the Navy, and for a while after I got out—when I was 25 and living started getting complicated."

Living stayed complicated until Robards made up his mind to follow what he called an "inward drive" to be an actor. He could not give in to this compulsion to act without a struggle, because he had been deeply unhappy over his father's shattered career.

"When I was little, my father was one of the biggest names in Hollywood," Robards said. "Suddenly—and how it happened to him was always a great mystery to me—he wasn't a star anymore; he was on the fringe. From the time I was 14 I was always conscious of a sense of worry, of terrific insecurity—agents, phony talk, the waits for the phone to ring. It's not what I considered living."

But the lure of the stage proved irresistible after all, and Robards Jr. entered the American Academy of Dramatic Arts (where Robards Sr. had studied in 1911) with his father's blessing.

"My father has the most tremendous personality and wonderful looks—he looks like Fredric March," Robards said. "Being his son was a little overwhelming at times—quite a lot like the way Jamie is overshadowed by his father."

After the Academy came the usual stints in summer stock and on the road, leading to the eventual meeting with Quintero. "I don't feel I've really started," Robards said, speaking of his current triumph with characteristic modesty. "There are plenty of places to go. I'd love to do *Moon for the Misbegotten* some day; it's really an extension of my present role—it's about Jamie a few years later. I'd also like to do some Shakespeare—and, of course, I'd like to go back to the Circle in the Square to do another play with José."

Jason Jamie Robards Tyrone

by Barbara Gelb

Barbara Gelb is co-author with Arthur Gelb of *O'Neill: Life with Monte Cristo* (Applause Books, 2000), a revised and expanded version of a biography considered a standard work since it first appeared in 1962. The following was published in *The New York Times Magazine*, January 20, 1974, and is reprinted with the kind permission of the author. Copyright © 1974 by the New York Times Co. Reprinted by permission.

The theater, being rooted in fantasy, is full of superstition and ghosts and wondrous coincidences, and people who work in the theater are more likely than other people to believe in such things as predetermination. Eugene O'Neill firmly believed in the Furies and he put them into his plays and was hounded by them in life, and Jason Robards, who has played tag with the Furies himself, feels that his spectacularly well-received arrival on Broadway as the middle-aged, dying Jamie Tyrone in O'Neill's *A Moon for the Misbegotten* has something fateful about it.

This is the third time that Robards has triumphantly played a character modeled on O'Neill's tragic older brother, Jamie—a man who haunted O'Neill all his life. Seventeen years ago, Robards played Hickey, a symbolic version of Jamie O'Neill, in the Off Broadway revival of *The Iceman Cometh*, and was instantly recognized as an extraordinarily talented actor with a striking affinity for O'Neill. Later that same season, at 34, he created the role of the 33-year-old Jamie Tyrone in *Long Day's Journey Into Night.*

Ever since then, Robards has wanted to play the older Jamie Tyrone, a man in his 40s. "I'd love to do *A Moon for the Misbegotten* some day—it's really an extension of my present role," he said when *Long Day's Journey* established him as a star. But the vicissitudes of the theater being what they are, and the Robards destiny being what it was, he was 51 before the chance presented itself. As it is, he barely made it. He had been living an O'Neillian life for a long time and an O'Neillian life is a life of cataclysm.

Robards understood the Jamie character, written by O'Neill "in tears and blood," because he had wept and bled himself. When he played the young Jamie in 1956, Robards was a complicated man, subject to depressions and fits of drunken rage. As Robards grew older, the depression grew deeper and the drinking more destructive. The O'Neill family had been plagued by alcoholism, and *The Iceman, Long Day's Journey* and *A Moon for the Misbegotten* are imbued with alcoholic guilt and despair. The O'Neill specter clung to Robards and finally, a little over a year ago, nearly engulfed him. He fell into what he now believes to have been a suicidal rage over losing the role of Hickey in the recently released movie version of *The Iceman*, and wound up in a horrendous automobile accident. It is double-edged irony that he survived, and that he is making his Broadway comeback in the O'Neill role he has so long yearned to play.

Robards today is at the top of his form. The standing, bravo-shouting opening-night ovation for *A Moon for the Misbegotten* will doubtless continue for months to come. Robards is playing, of course, with the actress who is ideal in the role of Josie Hogan, O'Neill's ultimate Earth Mother. The applause is for Colleen Dewhurst, too—and for the play's director, José Quintero. The combination of Robards, Dewhurst and Quintero with one of O'Neill's finest, and, certainly his most lyrical play, has brought about a true theater miracle.

Like Jamie O'Neill, Robards was the older of two sons born to a popular, handsome, hard-drinking, touring actor; like Jamie, he chose to rival his father by adopting an acting career; also like Jamie, he never recovered from a childhood sense of rejection by an absent mother, and he grew up, like Jamie, with ghosts in his eyes. All that, of course, was coincidence. But it was inevitable, given this common background, that Robards should recognize himself in Jamie, respond to his tragedy, and be inspired to interpret him on the stage with a depth and poignancy that could bring audiences cheering to their feet.

While Robards has made his reputation playing O'Neill, and is unquestionably our foremost O'Neillian actor, he is more than that. On the stage, he has been superb in any role that expressed a universal and elemental human tragedy, a role in which he took an emotional beating and, as has rather frequently been the case, a role in which emotional disharmony manifested itself by drunkenness. He salvaged Arthur Miller's flawed play, *After the Fall*; heightened the tragedy of Lillian Hellman's *Toys in the Attic*; created a sensitive portrait of F. Scott Fitzgerald in *The Disenchanted*; established a reputation for wry tragicomedy in *A Thousand Clowns*; and breathed new life into Clifford Odets' *The Country Girl*, a televised version of which will be shown in February.

On the screen, oddly enough, his most persuasive and engaging roles have been in a handful of sophisticated Westerns that were beset by distribution problems and failed to get proper attention. *The Ballad of Cable Hogue*, for example, highly praised by a few perceptive critics, disappeared after a mysteriously short run. In it, Robards demonstrated, as he rarely has been able to do on the screen, that in a role with some human dimension, and with a director (Sam Peckinpah) who understands his style, he is a very appealing movie actor.

But he is innately a man of the theater, and in this era of diminished live theater in America, he and George C. Scott are the only native Americans who have achieved the top rank that was exemplified in more vigorous theater times by John Barrymore and Alfred Lunt (Marlon Brando and Anthony Quinn could have been up there, if they had not abandoned the stage for the screen.)

Not long after having seen *Long Day's Journey Into Night*, playwright Howard Lindsay watched Robards enter the Players Club one night, and said, "I thought, when I saw you walk in, that I was seeing a young Edwin Booth." Booth was part of the O'Neill legend. In *Long Day's Journey*, the father, James Tyrone, dwells on his wasted talent, recalling the time when as a young and promising actor he played Iago to Booth's Othello. He, too, had been heralded as "a young Booth."

The O'Neill lifestyle in which Robards nestles half-apprehensively, half-cozily, was typified by the party he and Colleen Dewhurst jointly gave on the opening night of *A Moon for the Misbegotten*. Like O'Neill, Robards is ill at ease among the socially pretentious. O'Neill called them "poseurs" and Robards calls them "phonies." There were no glittering celebrities among the guests. At Robards' table were relatives, family, friends and his former psychoanalyst. At Dewhurst's were her agent and a group of black ex-convicts who have formed a street-acting troupe and whom she has taken under her wing. Quintero was there with some close friends. The play's producers were not invited. (They came anyway.)

O'Neill, who preferred the company of stevedores and gangsters and sailors, would probably have found even that gathering too high-toned. Robards, who enjoys family get-togethers and, for drinking companionship, a handful of fellow actors who are old friends, felt that the party had grown too big and formal for real cheer. Like O'Neill, he is mostly a quiet man, ill-equipped for small talk, bored with public preening and uncomfortable with the brittle surface of the so-called beautiful people. That was one of the reasons for the failure of his third marriage, to the glamorous and social Lauren Bacall.

Robards fell in love with O'Neill's work as a very young man. He had joined the Navy at 17, thinking to make it his career. World War II kept him at sea and at 22, shortly before engaging in the Philippines campaign, he found a copy of O'Neill's *Strange Interlude* in the ship's library. The dialogue impressed him and he began to think of an acting career.

His father, Jason Robards Sr., after a brief stage career had become a film actor. The young Robards had read screenplays but was unimpressed by them. Reading O'Neill gave him a glimpse of what real acting could be. Discharged from the Navy, he enrolled at the American Academy of Dramatic Arts and in 1946 went with his class to see *The Iceman Cometh*. James Barton was playing the role of Hickey as a middle-aged man with little luster, and the poor production put O'Neill on the shelf for a decade. Yet something in Hickey's character reached out to Robards and gripped him.

"I saw part of myself standing there in Hickey," he recalls. Playing the role 10 years later, Robards found himself possessed by it. It was then that his O'Neill identity took root on stage and began spilling over offstage. Robards, then 34, brought to Hickey a dimension that

O'Neill did not live to see. The revival, largely due to Robards' intuitive performance, began the restoration of O'Neill's reputation. Both Hickey's creator and Hickey's interpreter blazed with new light when Robards sailed jauntily onstage, straw-hatted, flashily dressed, eyes gleaming satanically, croaking the line, "And another little drink won't do us any harm!"

Hickey's complicated character revolves around his ambivalent relationship with his wife, Evelyn. He deludes himself that he loves her and pities her for her long-suffering efforts to forgive him for his waywardness. "I'd never have the guts to go back and be forgiven again," Hickey says, "and that would break Evelyn's heart because to her it would mean I didn't love her anymore." It turns out that he has murdered her—out of "pity."

During one performance, Robards was shocked to hear himself say "Eleanore," instead of "Evelyn." Eleanore was his first wife's name and his marriage was running into difficulties. Soon after, Robards resorted to divorce—not murder—but he seemed, more and more, to be living a life shadowed by the O'Neills.

At 46, Jamie O'Neill was dead of the effects of alcoholism. Robards, at 46, was finding his drinking increasingly unmanageable. Analysis helped some, and he quit drinking for a year. He started to drink again—sometimes convivially, and that was fine; sometimes to unwind after a performance, and that was necessary; sometimes to escape, which is the worst kind of drinking of all. He felt his career skidding, and he drank out of desperation. Both Eugene and Jamie O'Neill had been through all of those phases. As Hickey says, "I wrote the book." As Robards said during the run of Long Day's Journey, "Jamie is the kind of drunk I understand." The older Jamie he is now playing is a different kind of drunk, but he is no stranger to Robards either. The young Jamie used drink to hide behind. The older one cannot. He has come to see himself too clearly, and can use drink only to kill himself.

Robards' next four years were an uphill struggle for self rescue—more like Eugene, who gave up drinking, than like Jamie. It took a profound shock to bring Robards back—much as it had the playwright. O'Neill at 24 had believed himself to be dying of tuberculosis, self-inflicted by years of drinking and tramping. He regarded his recovery as a "rebirth." Robards, at 50, was in an accident that all but killed him.

He regards his survival, with awe, as a return from the dead. Although not born a Catholic, as O'Neill was, he has a deep sense of religion. He cannot define it, but he insists he has always been very religious.

"I often wonder about that sense of religious guilt O'Neill puts into his plays. I had that. I was raised as a Christian Scientist by my father—the guilts they put on you!"

It happened last December. The accident left his face shattered beyond recognition and, it was thought for a time, beyond repair.

Curtain down. Curtain up.

That is what the director, José Quintero, softly calls out from the auditorium, to mark the end of Act I and the start of Act 2, during rehearsals late in November of *A Moon for the Misbegotten*, which has four acts. Robards walks into the wings. He has no more lines until almost the end of Act 2 and can think of other things until then.

He is craggily handsome, silver-haired, and looks his age. It has little to do with the physical after effects of his accident. His face has been superbly patched together by a plastic surgeon who is internationally known as "the magician," and there are no visible scars. He now bears a striking resemblance to O'Neill, heightened by a new mustache that he grew to cover the one scar that would show. His age is in his eyes, hazel sometimes, a haunted pale green at others, a cavernous black when he is in a mood. And his age is in the sag of his body, the weariness in his voice, the downward droop of his mouth. But that is the offstage Robards. Onstage he can still project the tautness, the vitality, the mercurial change from gloom to manic wit, the controlled passion that stamped his signature on Hickey in 1956.

"It was my role," he says. "I couldn't believe they'd give it to someone else."

Recalling his initial shock at learning that *The Iceman Cometh* would be filmed without him, Robards starts off mildly. "Well, I guess they had a right to put Lee [Marvin] in the role." Pause. "Maybe they thought I wouldn't work for the low salary everyone got." Pause. "Christ, they should have known I'd do that part for nothing." Pause. "Maybe they thought I was unreliable."

Robards and his wife of two and a half years, the former Lois O'Connor, were living in a canyon about halfway between Los Angeles and Santa Monica, and Marvin lived 15 minutes away. As Robards recalls it, he ran into Marvin in Malibu. "Say, I'm working with a buddy of ours," Marvin said. The buddy was John Frankenheimer, who had directed Robards in the two-part television production of *For Whom the Bell Tolls*. Robards went home and began to brood. Why was Frankenheimer doing this to him? Why hadn't he at least called him with some sort of explanation?

Frankenheimer says, perfectly reasonably, that he wanted to do his own completely fresh version of the play. "I never considered anyone but Lee Marvin," he says. "I didn't want to do a copy of someone else's production. And I don't understand why Jason expected me to telephone. I didn't feel I owed him an explanation."

But Robards felt otherwise. "It was, at first, a quiet kind of anger," Lois Robards says. "It was not an enormous rage. He would mutter, 'Son of a bitch.' But he got angrier as the weeks went by. He was so mad—as though something had been stolen from him."

Robards insists that his life at that time was in a decided upward swing. He believed he had finally found the right woman. He and Lois had a year-old daughter; they lived on a cliff overlooking the sea, to which Robards has always been drawn, and he was working enough to keep financially solvent. He felt he had successfully faced being 50—Lois had invited 50 friends to a party and provided a fireworks display. ("I cried a little," Robards says. "It was beautiful.") He was soon to begin shooting *The Day of the Dolphin* with three of his "best buddies," Buck Henry, Mike Nichols and George C. Scott, and he and Lois were making plans to leave for location in the Bahamas. He was drinking less, sticking mainly to sherry and beer. "I wasn't hitting the hard stuff anymore," he says.

But the wound of losing Hickey continued to fester. An actor's ego is a precarious thing, and self-doubt always lurks close to the surface. "I suppose the psychoanalysts would say that Jason had his accident because of *Iceman*," Frankenheimer says. "Well, I refuse to feel responsible." Robards' analyst, Dr. Ferruccio di Cori, feels that Robards' sense of rejection contributed to the accident. "Jason is a very fragile person," he says.

On Dec. 9, two days before the filming of *The Iceman Cometh* began, Robards drove the 50 miles into Los Angeles to have lunch with his younger brother, Glenn. Jason and Glenn had never been close, and their relationship is marked by some of the ambivalence that O'Neill tended to dwell on in his portraits of himself and Jamie.

The three-hour meeting, during which they discussed family problems, had a somewhat jarring effect on Robards. Later he joined his friend Tom Runyon for dinner at a Los Angeles restaurant Runyon operates as a hobby. "I had clams and steak and drank some sherry," Robards says. "I wasn't drunk, but I was very tired. I'd been away from home since early in the morning."

It was about 1 in the morning when Robards got into his car, a Mercedes 190—"a classic car, in perfect condition, that I'd had for years"—to drive the 50 miles home. Runyon got into his own car, having agreed to follow Robards and stop off at his house to say hello to Lois. Robards loves driving, is skilled at it and knew the winding back road he planned to take "like the back of my hand." It wound through what Robards calls "this secret and wonderful canyon." He wore no seat belt.

The road ran along mountains on one side. On the other side, unguarded by a rail, was a drop of about 300 feet to the ocean. Landslides are a familiar occurrence in the area, and there had been several small ones in the past month. "You have to understand," Robards says, "that you just can't go more than 35 miles an hour on that road, or you'd fly off the side of the canyon.

"That's all I was going. I was on the last stretch, had done all the hairpin turns, and on the last turn—I hit it." Robards remembers very little after that, although he was, of course, told about it later. He does recall thinking, "Tom is following me—thank Christ."

It was Runyon who saved his life. Robards' car spun, then hit the mountain. The vibration from the impact was something like the whirling of a Waring Blender, with his head at the center of the whirl. His face bounced back from every surface inside the solidly built car. No glass was broken, but every bone in Robards' face was. His nose was splintered, both his cheekbones broken, his palate cracked, most of his teeth knocked out and a large section of his upper lip almost severed. It hung by a thread of skin. His leg was punctured and a part of one finger was cut off. Miraculously, he was not blinded.

Runyon drove Robards to the Santa Monica Hospital. "I found out later I had something called chemical pneumonia," Robards says. "I had vomited into my lungs and was choking to death." By the time he reached the hospital, his heart had stopped beating. "I was dead," he says, still awed by the memory a year later.

By pure chance, the hospital had on its staff one of the world's leading plastic surgeons. Dr. Butler (a fictitious name, used at the doctor's request) received a call from Robards' internist shortly after 3 on Saturday morning. A tracheotomy was performed to alleviate the lung congestion, the heart was revived, and then, though it was precarious to perform further surgery, the lip was stitched into place; delay would have guaranteed its loss.

When Lois Robards first saw her husband, she was appalled. "His head was blown up like a balloon," she says. "His eyes were swollen shut, and he had the tube in his throat. He couldn't speak, of course. All I could think to do was say, 'Jason, I love you.'"

He was in intensive care for 10 days. At first he could only marvel at having escaped from death. Then, he waited tensely to know if the lip would take life; lip skin is impossible to replace by graft and permanent disfigurement seemed a very strong possibility. Dr. Butler was not optimistic. He tried to joke with Robards about it. "You've got a good hole there," he said. "From now on, the thing to do is play cigar parts." Robards thought that was very funny. After five days, the lip was secure. But Robards could not speak for two weeks, and he communicated with Lois and his doctors by scrawled notes. He wondered if he had permanently damaged his voice box, as well as his looks. One of the notes he scrawled to Lois was, "Have I got what Jack the Hawk had?" He was referring to the English actor, Jack Hawkins, who had temporarily lost his voice because of cancer of the throat.

Robards was in the hospital for a little over a month. Lois brought their baby daughter, Shannon, to visit him on Christmas day. His recovery, after having his face bones set, jaws wired, teeth replaced and cosmetic surgery performed, was more rapid than his doctors had thought possible.

"I'm a fast healer," Robards says.

"Do you believe it? The bum is working," Dr. Butler said on hearing that Robards was making a movie shortly after leaving the hospital.

Curtain down. Curtain up.

Robards felt himself to be truly on the mend, emotionally, as well as physically, about six months after his accident. The calm came from the same source as the tempest—O'Neill. He was invited to do a summer engagement of *A Moon for the Misbegotten* with José Quintero, the director who had discovered him. Quintero himself has not been unaffected by association with O'Neill. He has one thing in common with O'Neill that Robards does not—a Catholic-mystic background—and regards the playwright as his "spiritual father." "If Jason nearly died because of O'Neill," Quintero says, "O'Neill also saved his life."

Robards attributes the healing as much to Quintero as to O'Neill. In a way, the two are inseparable. "As soon as I started working with José, the anger started to go away," Robards says. "He put me at ease."

It was a kind of fateful timing that enabled Quintero to be of use to Robards in the summer of 1973. He had recently recovered from a period of artistic and personal depression, characterized, as with O'Neill and Robards, by flight into alcohol. Now he had quit drinking completely and forever.

A Moon for the Misbegotten was enthusiastically received in its limited run outside Chicago last June and July. The production had an unexpected blessing in Ed Flanders who, some years the junior of both Robards and Colleen Dewhurst, played the role of Josie Hogan's father with a wicked Irish wit that would have enchanted O'Neill. Word of the production's success filtered back East, and money was found to produce it, first at the Kennedy Center in Washington and then on Broadway. *A Moon for the Misbegotten* was proving to be a cathartic event all around.

Curtain down. Curtain up.

The summer cast, which disbanded and engaged in other projects during the next five months, reassembled in New York toward the end of November. Quintero called the first formal rehearsal on Nov. 27 on the stage of the Morosco. More rattling of ghostly bones. Nov. 27 turned out to be the 20th anniversary of O'Neill's death. It also turned out that the Morosco was where O'Neill had his first full-length play produced on Broadway—*Beyond the Horizon*, in 1920. O'Neill's actor father, James, finally reconciled with O'Neill after years of conflict, sat in a box to watch the play. At its end, he said to his son, tears streaming down his cheeks, "Are you trying to send the audience home to commit suicide?"

Robards' actor father had died 10 years ago. He had not gotten along with his son either over the years, but they were reconciled when

Robards Sr. came to see Jason several times in *Long Day's Journey Into Night*, once watching the whole performance from the wings.

Robards was dressed jauntily for the rehearsal of *A Moon for the Misbegotten*. He wore well-cut tan trousers with a slight flair at the cuffless bottom, a tan bush jacket, a red velour shirt; he had arrived in a plaid, Sherlock Holmes hat that matched his plaid wool topcoat. There is still much of the Jamie in him. O'Neill describes Jamie in *Moon* as having "the ghost of a former youthful, irresponsible Irish charm—that of the beguiling ne'er-do-well, sentimental and roman-tic. It is his humor and charm which have kept him attractive to women and popular with men as a drinking companion."

Clearly, Robards, like Jamie, is attractive to women. Four of them have married him. He and Lauren Bacall, by whom he has a 10-year-old named Sam, are still good friends. He is also good friends with his first wife, Eleanore, who is the mother of three of his children—Jason 3d, 24, Sarah, 22, and David, 16. He is not good friends with his second wife, Rachel, to whom he was married very briefly, but whom he has been supporting, with displeasure, ever since.

Lois Robards, to whom he has been married nearly four years, is a slim, elegant, perceptive woman, 14 years younger than Robards. "She boosts me up," he says. Lois is one of eight sisters, and her fam-ily has always been closely knit. "For the first time in my life, I belong to a family," Robards says.

"Jason cares more about himself now," Lois says.

Though he drinks less, Robards is still, like Jamie, a popular drinking companion—of such as Christopher Plummer, Peter O'Toole, and George C. Scott. He calls them "Chrissy," "Tooley O'Pete," and "G. C." As for the humor and charm, those are among his most viable qualities onstage and off. The charm, however, is only part Irish. There are equal parts of Welsh and English, and a smidgeon of Swedish.

He still has, in common with Jamie, mixed feelings toward his mother. Those tangled feelings surfaced during early rehearsals of *A Moon for the Misbegotten*. Robards found himself choking over some lines in a long, anguished monologue that is the play's fulcrum. Jamie is describing his mother's death and his fury at having been abandoned by her. The fury, unrealistic in terms of a middle-aged man's loss of his elderly mother, is a displacement of Jamie's childhood sense of abandonment. The real Jamie had discovered as a boy that his mother was a morphine addict. That aspect of the relationship is relentlessly explored in *Long Day's Journey*, and it is one that Robards has had ample opportunity to reflect upon. "Do you realize that Jamie talks directly to his mother only once in the entire play?" he says.

The Act 3 lines which Robards kept choking on during rehearsal: "...her body in a coffin with her face made up. I couldn't hardly recognize her. She looked young and pretty like someone I remembered meeting long ago. Practically a stranger. To whom I was a stranger. Cold and indifferent. Not worried about me anymore. Free at last. Free from worry. From pain. From me...." And later he adds: "It was as if I wanted revenge—because I'd been left alone ... because no one was left who could help me."

The lines make more emotional sense when construed as the words of an abandoned child, rather than those of an aging, if bereaved, adult. And that explains why Robards, whose mother is very much alive, reacted to them as he did. He actually found himself crying during one rehearsal—"Much too early," he says. Later in the act, he is called on to sob at some length.

Ella O'Neill had withdrawn into a drugged world, where her children could not reach her. Unable to cope herself, and with her husband often on tour, she sent both of her sons, barely past infancy, to boarding schools.

Hope Robards was divorced from her husband when Jason was 5 and his brother was 1. She remarried, and resigned her children's care to their father. He, being often on tour, placed them, barely past infancy, in a boarding school.

Robards, offstage, speaks of his mother calmly and tolerantly. Lois Robards is less tolerant. "We spent a recent Thanksgiving with Jason's mother," she says. "I was horrified to find it was the first Thanksgiving they'd spent together in 27 years. I was afraid to ask how many Christmases they'd spent together."

Curtain down. Curtain up.

Ironically, the movie version of *The Iceman Cometh*, released at the end of October [1973], has done much to enhance Robards's reputation. Many reviews of the film, justly laudatory in every other respect, mentioned the absence of Robards and compared Lee Marvin's performance unfavorably with his in the play. Dozens of friends called Robards after reading the reviews. The gist of their comment was,

"Those are the best notices you've ever had." The reviews were not as good as those for *A Moon for the Misbegotten*, which were unqualified raves.

At home in a rented town house a few days after the opening, Robards is relaxed and, for him, expansive. His eyes have the old, mischievous Jamie gleam, and the glow of success has smoothed the tension from his face and subtracted several years from his age. He consumes a lot of coffee and smokes a great deal. He seems to have made up his mind to drink only for relaxation. ("That's swell," said a friend who drank with him after a recent performance, "but get yourself a chauffeur.")

Lois Robards is a soothing presence, trim in a sweater and jeans, her long, light brown hair coiled in a bun. She answers all phone calls, screens invitations and allows Shannon O'Connor Robards to be visible in small and entertaining doses. Shannon is blonde, juicy, vocal, in perpetual motion and full of feminine guile.

"I'll be 70 when she's 21," Robards says, "but I intend to be around to take her down the aisle."

His reaction to his success is, he says, surprise. "Audiences must be starving for meaningful theater," he says. "They are responding to this as though it's a new play."

What next? Can Robards play anything as successfully as he can play O'Neill? Perhaps not quite as successfully, he admits.

There is one role he is particularly eager to play, that of Cornelius Melody in *A Touch of the Poet*, a character O'Neill modeled on his father. Robards was to have done Melody on television this month with Quintero, but had to withdraw because the strain of simultaneously playing two very demanding O'Neill heroes proved too taxing for his voice and his psyche. Quintero also withdrew, because he will not direct the play with anyone but Robards. (The television producers are suing both Robards and Quintero for breach of contract.) They will probably do the play, instead, on Broadway, after the run of *A Moon for the Misbegotten*. Robards also hopes, one day, to play the father in *Long Day's Journey*. If he had his choice, he would like to perform in a season of O'Neill repertory. He would particularly like to revive *The Iceman Cometh*, for Hickey is still his favorite of all the O'Neill roles. He would also like to revive O'Neill's long one-acter, *Hughie*, in which he appeared 10 years ago. And he has been trying for several years to get backing for a musical about Junius Brutus Booth, the alcoholic father of Edwin and John Wilkes.

What about Shakespeare, with whom Robards has not, to date, been too successful? "Of course I want to do more of Billy Big Boy," Robards says. "I'm too old now to play Hamlet, but I'd like to try Lear."

Dr. di Cori, who uses psychodrama in therapy and has analyzed Robards' acting as well as his personality, feels Robards is not empathetic to Shakespeare. "But does that really matter?" he says. "What's wrong with being the greatest living O'Neill actor?"

What indeed? Laurence Olivier, certainly one of the greatest Shakespearean actors, was disappointing when he played O'Neill. His recent portrayal of James Tyrone in *Long Day's Journey Into Night* failed to catch O'Neill's earthy, Irish-American rhythms. He was brave to try it, and it was a tribute to our only Nobel Prize–winning playwright, and Olivier is still the untouchable.

Robards will bravely try more Shakespeare, and perhaps one day he will even master Lear. But it doesn't really matter. There is nothing very wrong with being the leading interpreter of our own greatest dramatist, and Robards is that, for all foreseeable seasons.

A Meeting with the Redoubtable Jason

by Edward L. Shaughnessy

Edward Shaughnessy is Professor Emeritus of English at Butler University in Indianapolis. His most recent book is *Down the Nights and Down the Days: Eugene O'Neill's Catholic Sensibility* (University of Notre Dame Press, 1997). His important research into the lives of "Ella, James, and Jamie O'Neill" was published in *The Eugene O'Neill Review* in the Fall 1991 issue, pp. 5–92.

By 1930, Eugene O'Neill had developed something beyond the character-range of the mere journeyman dialogist. What he needed, of course, were actors capable of bringing his characters to life. Only three, he said, had achieved exactly what he had hoped to achieve: Charles Gilpin in *The Emperor Jones*, Louis Wolheim in *The Hairy Ape,* and Walter Huston in *Desire Under the Elms.*

If he could have seen the 1956 revival of *The Iceman Cometh*, however, O'Neill would surely have placed Jason Robards in that pantheon, a man whose background and experiences so uncannily paralleled his own. That would have been fitting and proper. For, as things turned out, Robards was one of the dozen or so women and men who restored O'Neill forever to his rightful station as America's premiere dramatist.

If ever a man lived by another's words, it was Jason, who spoke O'Neill's truth. But, to understand this phenomenon, we must first put the background into focus, for the life we celebrate in these memoirs represents an instance of theater heroism as splendid as any we may ever know.

Like O'Neill, whose plays gave his career direction and meaning, Jason Robards was a son of the theater. Yet theirs was a theater fractured in the cosmos quake of the twentieth century. Shakespeare's "mirror up to nature," by then a spiderweb of cracks, reflected only a broken world. Thus, their fathers' theater of easy optimism and formula melodrama spoke to them with little authority. Steeped in the faithlessness of the new day, they were forced to wonder how their talents should be spent; how their art and craft might achieve nobility.

The modern playwright who has sought to master his total art form has had to confront an especially difficult issue. Was it even possible any longer to represent men and women as tragic figures? Indeed, did there remain a language fit to pursue the classic genre? These questions are philosophical and historical, religious and cultural. They have been endlessly debated, of course, and will not soon be solved.

In 1941 O'Neill's inveterate defender, Joseph Wood Krutch, spoke to both sides of the issue: that is, to the prospects for modern tragedy and to the question of language:

> To find in the play [*Mourning Becomes Electra*] any lack at all one must compare it with the very greatest works of dramatic literature, but when one does compare it with *Hamlet* or *Macbeth,* one realizes that it does lack just one thing and that thing is language—words as thrilling as the action which accompanies them.

In 1949 Arthur Miller spoke to the question: "I believe that the common man is as apt a subject for tragedy in its highest sense as kings were." Critics on the side of tradition would, no doubt, disagree with Miller's view (e.g., Francis Fergusson); modernists, I think, would assent (e.g., Gerald Weales). This is certain, however: many theater historians consider the phrase "modern dramatic tragedy" to be something of an oxymoron.

If this situation has created a major dilemma for playwrights of the twentieth century, it may nonetheless have worked to the advantage of Jason Robards. With his bourbon-and-smoke-cured voice,

Robards made a sound too gravelly for lordly Shakespearean types (although he might have made an impressive Macbeth). His portrayals evoked the air of one deeply dyed in the vat of cynicism, a soul rubbed raw by personal shakes and shudders. Consider: wasn't Robards' voice perfectly pitched to answer the question put by the Night Clerk in *Hughie*? "What's the truth?" And the hapless Erie Smith responds, "Nothing, Pal. Not a thing." His was a modern range: he could kid with or enrage the "Brothers and Sisters" of the lower precincts; he could wound and be wounded by Mama, Papa and the Kid; he might wince at the slatternly Nora and insult the lick-spittles, Roche and Riley.

I

Even if O'Neill was limited in language, however, his words and rhythms fit perfectly many of the characters he created, often the down-and-outs or the otherwise defeated. O'Neill's creations also included his "higher" types: the stammering lyricists, Edmund Tyrone and Richard Miller; the sensitive poet-architect, Dion Anthony; the brittle intellectual, Charles Marsden; and the taut New Englander, Lavinia Mannon.

Robards never sat for portraits of Edmund, Richard, Dion, Marsden, or many another character in the O'Neill gallery. Indeed, his career record includes no work in *Desire Under the Elms, Strange Interlude*, or *Mourning Becomes Electra*, all major entries in the O'Neill canon. Some may wonder whence, then, this widely heralded identification with Eugene O'Neill? Indeed, with the exception of Nat Miller (the George M. Cohan part) in *Ah, Wilderness!* (1933), Jason Robards never took a role in an O'Neill play of the early or middle periods. He might very well have made a splendid Captain Keeney or Ephraim Cabot.

Yet I say without hesitation that O'Neill would have included Robards among his company of acting elite. Jason had made his first important mark in the theater as the iceman Hickey and he stopped the world with his performance. This play demands an actor who can render justice to those O'Neill loved: "The people in that saloon were the best friends I've ever known.... Their weakness was not an evil. It is a weakness found in all men." Hickey's misguided mission was to save them, even as he was one of them. O'Neill needed a great actor, and he got one: the redoubtable Mr. Robards. Jason belonged on the boards—with Ralph Richardson and Fredric March; with Colleen Dewhurst and Ed Flanders; with Geraldine Fitzgerald and Zoe Caldwell. He belonged.

The year 1956 was truly an *annus mirabilis* in the life of Jason Robards. From May through November he played in nearly 200 of the 565 consecutive performances of *The Iceman Cometh*; Leo Penn replaced him, but Jason created the definitive Hickey. Then, on November 7th of that year he opened as James Tyrone, Jr., in *Long Day's Journey Into Night* and thus helped to launch its run of 390 consecutive performances. These tandem achievements in two of the modern theater's most challenging roles constitute something beyond *tour de force*. They stand as a feat of endurance and longevity that fairly defies belief.

At any rate, his notices in 1956–57 raise another fascinating question: What is the nature of Robards' kinship with certain O'Neill parts? Playing the fifty-year-old Hickey and the Jamie of 33, when he himself was only 34, required that he maintain a remarkable psychological balance. He became first the working-class wife-slayer and then the well-educated New Englander and ne'er-do-well.

At the moment I can offer a mere, and confessedly inadequate, notion as to how the formidable Mr. Robards managed all this. But everything suggests that he gained, somehow, a wide-ranging knowledge of the guilt manifestations that operate in human relationships. The layman can offer no just critique except to grant that the actor gained a kind of *experiential knowledge* from living, in rapid succession, the "lives" of Theodore Hickman and Jamie Tyrone. It may be that such a chameleon suppleness was demanded of over-the-road men from another time who played the classical repertoire (the Booths, Barrymores, and James O'Neill, the elder). But an extended run as Hickey or one of the Tyrones calls for an expense of psychic energy of a different magnitude.

In any case, the audience probably cares little how the actor achieves the insights that move him or her. When the curtain goes up, what we want is a professional performance. The actor's problem is how to maintain an evenness of quality over weeks and months. Kevin Spacey, himself a pretty fair Hickey, remarked at the time of Robards' death, "He had no patience for the self-analysis that some indulged in. He was not interested in the psychology of acting. His view of acting was just do it. Learn it. Serve it" (*NY Times*, 1-14-01). In formula this might well read: *performance + knowledge + dedication.* Jason served with such conviction that all who beheld it could believe in the truth of his work.

Every account of Robards, especially the Robards of 1956–1973, suggests that he was a man of deep psychological complexity. This nature probably contributed, not only to the development of his Hickey, but also made possible his investing, with similar dynamics, Erie Smith, the fast-talking sport of *Hughie* (1964). Further, Robards undoubtedly gained equally profound insights from playing Jamie in *Long Day's Journey.* This depth of understanding, I do believe, made credible Jim Tyrone's final unburdening to Josie Hogan, his confessor in *A Moon for the Misbegotten* (1973). Indeed, these experiences caused Robards, eventually, to yearn for the part of James Tyrone, Sr., a part that would give him "total" knowledge of that astonishing O'Neillian portrait of the father-son relationship.

II

Veteran Irish director Sean Cotter is my source for the fact that in the fifties and sixties Peter O'Toole considered Robards coequal fine actor and sleuth unrivalled in locating the still-extant saloons O'Neill had once haunted. They had many a hilarious adventure together, Cotter said. But, from a brief meeting with him, I know that Mr. Robards recalled those days with mixed sadness and nostalgia, the bittersweet remainders.

In March of 1974 I travelled to New York to see the highly acclaimed production of *A Moon for the Misbegotten.* This was well along into the O'Neill revival but still some years before the founding of the Eugene O'Neill Society (1979). The play had flopped when it was first presented by the Theatre Guild in Columbus and closed shortly thereafter in St. Louis (1947). That failure had followed by only a few months the lukewarm reception of *The Iceman Cometh* on Broadway (October 1946). As the late Travis Bogard observed, "[*A Moon for the Misbegotten*] is doomed to failure without superb acting." And that is what it got in 1973–74.

I had read most of the glowing reviews, including those by Clive Barnes and Walter Kerr. But for a total and unqualified encomium, nothing I had come upon compared with T. E. Kalem's tribute in *Time Magazine*:

> Broadway is a noble word again. Power, beauty, passion and truth command the stage of the Morosco Theater where *A Moon for the Misbegotten* has been revived in unmitigated triumph. We owe it all to the sensitive direction of José Quintero, the matchless performances of Jason Robards, Colleen Dewhurst and Ed Flanders and the piercing vision of Eugene O'Neill....

Jason Robards and Colleen Dewhurst in *A Moon for the Misbegotten*, 1973–1974. Copyright © 1974 by Martha Swope and TimePix. Used by permission of Martha Swope/TimePix. P.

> Over the years, Jason Robards' psychic affinity for O'Neill has marked the peaks of his acting career. His Hickey in *The Iceman Cometh*, Jamie in *Long Day's Journey*, and title role in *Hughie* [sic] will probably never be surpassed. Increasingly, Robards even looks like O'Neill. He has the brooding, deep-set eyes that look out from O'Neill's photographs with searing gravity. His performance in *Misbegotten* will remain a touchstone for all actors to measure themselves by. [January 14, 1974, p. 42]

"Get thee to the Morosco," I said to myself.

III

I'm not certain if the house was full. That now-razed theater had a capacity of 500–600. Even for this Wednesday matinee, however, given all the testimonies to the cast's high achievement, I doubt if there was an empty seat in the building. Of course, I knew very well that the Morosco had hosted *Beyond the Horizon* in 1920. (Which was the greater joy to O'Neill, I wondered: that his father and mother were in a box on opening night; or that the play won him a first Pulitzer Prize? [His father would die that summer.]) With a seat, front-row center, I felt favored by the gods.

I chatted with him, for half an hour or so, in his dressing room, a conversation it is altogether unlikely that he recalled ever again. More on that exchange. Here is how the opportunity developed.

I had been in Broadway houses before, but attendance on the main stem was not a typical Hoosier overnight. Not all went well. I had taken a Trailways' bus to New York. Somewhere near Pittsburgh, the driver, mistaking the air-conditioner control for the heater, could not reverse the maneuver. It was March; we were still some 400 miles from the Port Authority Building. Thus I arrived at the Morosco with a severe chill but was to be yet further tested. Seated next to me was a somewhat original type, a tall young man with a raspy cough. This was not too serious by itself, but every few minutes he would yawn or make a low moan and then, in a violent jolt, thrust himself forward as he shifted his weight from one side to the other. Completing this acrobatic maneuver, he would exhale a depressurizing *"Ahhaaaa."* Once, Robards himself directed a baleful glance in our direction, a gesture that is not scripted. (I know I saw the flicker of a smile cross Ed Flanders' lips.) Maybe the young man, at a certain point, tired of the dialogue (or of my muttering, "May ye suffer the unending fires"). He left at intermission, the company relieved, I was sure.

Josie Hogan appeared immediately. The house broke out in applause as Colleen Dewhurst, the farmer's daughter, sprinted onto the stage *sans* footwear, *"more powerful than any but an exceptionally strong man."* We were off. At once she begins to abuse her brother Mike, a pious and humorless teetotaler who'd have no hope in this life to match the venom-tongued Jim Tyrone. Yet a sisterly side of Josie was also revealed, something pulled from the late Colleen's storehouse of theatrical acumen. Anyone who has read the script knows that these two sides of her nature repeatedly surface as she spars with her father, the bantam but formidable Phil Hogan, another "wily Mick" who can throw darts at all comers with a velocity nearly the equal of Josie's. It's all great fun.

Enter the landlord, Tyrone.

IV

The challenge of playing Jim Tyrone is suggested in the stage directions: *"a certain Mephistophelian quality, habitually cynical expression, the ghost of a former youthful, irresponsible Irish charm, [a] humor and charm which have kept him attractive to women, and popular with men as a drinking companion."* Here may be an assemblage of traits no mortal can project. Robards, who could be a deft comedian, does not come on stage until halfway through the first act. He was the nearly perfect practitioner of sardonic humor, no easy assignment, even for a veteran who has honed his skills over many years.

O'Neill, his comedian's talents often overlooked, felt that in *The Iceman Cometh* he had created some very funny lines. He matched these in *Moon*, another of the late tragedies. Of course, he knew every verbal pratfall from vaudeville. Take, for example, the side-splitting scene in which Josie and Phil fluster the stuffy T. Stedman Harder, the Standard Oil millionaire whose estate abuts Hogan's lowly farm. The tricks employed to outrage Harder are taken, without blushes, from the turn-of-the-century bag of comic devices.

By the time he wrote the late masterpieces, O'Neill had sloughed off most of the experimental props that had served to telegraph his intentions: asides, soliloquies, masks, symbolic scenery. He had come to rely on two things: his own profound knowledge of his characters' psychology and the actors' sense of his (the playwright's) understanding. This is why, I think, O'Neill is often found wanting and seems clumsy to many critics and playgoers. They do not understand that, in the theater of his own mind, O'Neill knew that only fine actors could do what he asks. And this is also why, when lesser directors choose lesser actors, the challenge cannot be met. And the play "fails."

I invoke again Bogard's admonition that without fine acting in the parts of Josie and Jim *A Moon for the Misbegotten* will not only fail but will be considered a poor play. The actors must possess, if you will, a certain co-naturality with their characters. In Ireland I found broad evidence of O'Neill's popularity among actors. Again and again they saw him as an American theatrical giant and practically begged to be involved in his plays. These included Sean Cotter, Vincent Dowling, Siobhan McKenna, and many others in the Republic; Stella McCusker, Liam O'Callaghan, and the late Jack McQuoid in the North. O'Neill was not especially well received in the literature departments of Irish universities.

As the late Ms. Dewhurst remarked in "A Glory of Ghosts," a PBS documentary on O'Neill in 1986, "The more you play a [great] play, the more you realize what's inside of it ... about life." Something of this could be understood in several instances of the Morosco production I saw. For example, as the play moves toward its bleak revelations in late Act III, not all humor is lost; but its lightness is. And, as Jim's darker and darker thoughts come on in the buildup to his confession, Jason's genius is fully exhibited.

Tyrone labors under a heavier and heavier load of accruing remorse and sorrow. But Jason himself did not fall off stride as an actor, even as his character descends into an abyss of despair. And as he undergoes a deeper and deeper self-bruising, Jim's cynical defenses assault his spirit; his humor, ever more lethal and sardonic, carries forward. When, after a brief withdrawal, Josie returns with a bottle of Phil's best bonded bourbon, Jim says he's "been dying of loneliness." But his humor does not lighten his burden of guilt.

Josie. You'll die of lying some day. But I'm glad you're alive again. I thought when I left you really were dying on me.

Tyrone. No such luck [emphasis mine].

Colleen Dewhurst made another acute judgment. "O'Neill," she said, "gives you no safety net." She meant that you'd better understand the words because there is nothing else to support you. That fine acting is an art, O'Neill knew well. The words are the writer's, but the actors' capacity, born of talent *and* experience, is equally a mystery. Quintero realized this. After Robards had, years earlier, proved to José his own equal understanding of O'Neill by evoking a fully credible Hickey, Quintero knew he also had the *Moon's* Jim Tyrone. By then the director had gained the confidence to identify other first-line actors. Hence his choice of Colleen Dewhurst to play Josie.

If playing Jim Tyrone was a labor of love, it was still hard work. From my station, front-row middle, I could sometimes hear Robards breathe and observe droplets of sweat on his brow and upper lip. Those who know the play will remember that as Act II ends, Tyrone, thinking of seducing Josie, is left alone on the stage: *"His hand is trembling so violently he cannot light the cigarette."* The audience participates in his tension. *Curtain.* After an interval of fifteen–twenty minutes the house lights dim again, while *"Tyrone is still trying with shaking hands to get his cigarette lighted."* Show people call this "stage business." Done properly, it is the sign of a professional actor.

The actor must by now be, as it were, inside the skin and brain of Jim Tyrone—and have retained his motivation throughout the interval. If we think, "These are the easy moments, feigning fear or garbling one's words," we fail the test of worthy spectatorship. Attention must be paid. Yet, it must be granted, *A Moon for the Misbegotten* and *The Iceman Cometh* are not fare for adolescents, who will more easily understand *Hamlet*. The dialogue will seem like self-absorbed and drunken drivel to spectators unprepared to do their share of the work. But what exquisite enjoyment for those who join in the characters' conflicts.

And if we think that carrying off the stage business is a piece of cake, add into the equation the "outside" stresses that increase the actor's difficulty. The house is full of theater *cognoscenti*; the most discerning drama critics of the theater establishment are sprinkled throughout the house. Here is what Jason communicated: that, once again, Jim Tyrone has come to fear his own capacity to spoil something good. This realization is produced via the same logic O'Neill invoked when Jamie taunts Edmund in *Long Day's Journey*. How fortunate we are to have the film record of Jason Robards' execution in the part of Jamie, a remarkable blending of love and hate, the very crystallizing of ambivalence. Robards' achievement in this family tragedy is a moment of greatness now preserved forever:

Want to warn you—against me. Mama and Papa are right. I've been rotten bad influence. And worst of it is. I did it on purpose.... Did it on purpose to make a bum of you.... I love you more than I hate you…. But you'd better be on your guard. Because I'll do my damnedest to make you fail. Can't help it. I hate myself. Got to take revenge. On everyone else. Especially you.

To carry out such an assignment is a challenge too great for many actors. "No sweat!" they may say. The mediocre actor will not even recognize the difficulty of what he is asked to do. But I tell you, there is sweat. I saw it on Robards' face in the part of Jim Tyrone. Frightened by the potential evil in his own soul, he gives signs of preparation for confession. But he, who was not raised in O'Neill's (rejected) faith, had by this time absorbed Eugene's sensibility. Jason clearly understood the guilt and remorse with which O'Neill has impacted and charged his characters.

"O'Neill gives you no safety net." That is, either one believes in the truth of the character's lines or one doesn't. Jason believed in O'Neill's words.

V

The performance was over. Jim Tyrone has walked off into a new day, absolved by Josie's benediction: "May you have your wish and die in your sleep soon, Jim, darling. May you rest forever in forgiveness and peace." *Curtain*: thunderous applause, encores. Slowly, the house emptied. After several minutes, I noticed two people walking down the right side aisle: Henry Fonda and his statuesque wife. They were going backstage. I sat for some minutes, trying to etch into memory the contours of the stage and set. The recollection remains intact, some twenty-seven years later.

Soon, Jason's dresser, H. R. Donnelly, walked the Fondas to the street door. As he returned, I made bold to ask: "Would it be possible to say hello to Mr. Robards?" Chances seemed small, the next performance to be given at 8:00 o'clock. "Wait." In thirty seconds, he returned. "Follow me. He'll see you." This was about 4:00 P.M. I was with Jason until about 4:25.

Back stage was cluttered. Unwrapped pipes showed everywhere. Mr. Robards' room was a bit cramped. He rose to greet me, as I praised the production and performances by the three principals. The actor seemed glad to see me, a stranger from the hinterland.

All O'Neillians recall Jason's long fight against severe alcoholism.

After he had conquered the illness, he gained a kind of second identity by doing a television service announcement: "I'm living proof that you don't have to die for a drink." This may have referred to the disastrous automobile accident he had on a canyon highway one night in December 1972.

Robards had been filled with resentment against John Frankenheimer, who had cast Lee Marvin in the part of Hickey in a film version of *The Iceman Cometh*. The actor, then age fifty, thought the part was *his*. The accident all but killed him and nearly ended his career; he was, in fact, pronounced dead at the Santa Monica Hospital, with every bone in his face smashed and major internal injuries. In the hospital Jason was rescued by a plastic surgeon so skilled that his colleagues called him "the magic man." Thereafter, the only evidence of surgery was at the point where his upper lip had had to be sewn back on. He now wore a mustache to cover that scar. (A detailed account of all this is Barbara Gelb's "Jason Jamie Robards Tyrone," *New York Times Magazine*, 1/20/74.)

By the time *Moon* opened at the Morosco in late December 1973, Jason had established a promising new life. His wife of four years, Lois O'Connor, and their daughter, Shannon, gave Jason Robards every reason to recover. Added to this was his collaboration with an energized José Quintero.

He sat at his dressing table, I in a chair across from him. He seemed in no way "winded" from the afternoon's work and said he was looking forward to the repeat performance that evening. After a few minutes, Donnelly came in to say that he would bring in a snack at 5:30; Jason would rest after I left.

We chatted, mainly about Eugene and Jamie. He said he hoped, someday, to play the elder James Tyrone. He had enjoyed very much working with Ralph Richardson, a "worthy mentor." There was no mention by either of us of Frankenheimer or Lee Marvin, who had long been his pals.

"Where are you from, what do you do?" I smiled and said, "I'm from Indiana," aware that we both took an insider's delight in the coincidence. Hickey remarks to "de gang" that he learned his trade as the son of a circuit-riding preacher:

> It's in my blood, I guess. My old man used to whale salvation into my heinie with a birch rod. He was a preacher in the sticks of Indiana,

like I've told you. I got my knack of sales gab from him, too. He was the boy who could sell those Hoosier hayseeds building lots along the Golden Street!

Jason laughed too. "Well," he said, "I guess they got the gospel out to the frontier." I asked him to sign my program. He'd be glad to but didn't have anything at hand. "All I have," I said, "is a pen with teacher's red ink." He wrote, "To Ed Shaughnessy, in teacher's red ink, not Scotch."

I thanked him and left. Down the street I stopped in a bar to scribble some notes about my afternoon at the Morosco. I knew that I would not soon forget Jason's kindness and his reflections on O'Neill. But the image of another actor came to mind as well: yes, another actor who had loved Eugene. I thought of all three men and silently repeated James O'Neill's favorite toast: "To sunny days and starry nights."

Quintero Directs Robards in A Touch of the Poet

by Edwin J. McDonough

> The following, excerpted from McDonough's *Quintero Directs O'Neill* (Chicago: A Cappella Books, 1991), is reprinted with the permission of author and publisher. All quotations not otherwise attributed are from interviews conducted by the author. Mr. McDonough performed in two of Quintero's O'Neill productions.

The out-of-town collapse of *A Moon for the Misbegotten* in 1947 influenced Eugene O'Neill to delay production of *A Touch of the Poet*, "even though Robert Edmond Jones had already drawn preliminary sketches for the set and plans had been formulated to have either Spencer Tracy or Laurence Olivier portray Con Melody."[1] O'Neill was fully aware of the difficulty of casting the part. He told George Jean Nathan that "what this one needs is an actor like Maurice Barrymore or James O'Neill, my old man. One of those big-chested, chiseled-mug, romantic old boys."[2] In 1950, Lawrence Langner requested that O'Neill agree to a production "with a certain director of whom he approved. 'I don't believe I could live through a production of a new play right now,' he replied, and to my protestation that we would do everything possible to make things easy for him, he answered, 'No, that's my last word on the subject.'"[3]

The play finally had its American premiere in New York on October 2, 1958, at the Helen Hayes Theatre on West 46th Street. Harold Clurman directed the production that was produced by Robert Whitehead under the auspices of the Producers' Theatre. The production received excellent notices and ran for 284 performances. It is famous in theatrical circles for the lack of chemistry among Eric Portman's British Con, Kim Stanley's Actors' Studio Sara, and Helen Hayes' sweetness-and-light Nora.

In 1973, José Quintero had contracted to direct Jason Robards in a Theatre-in-America television production of *A Touch of the Poet*. Robards knew the 1958 production well because he was a close friend of cast members Kim Stanley, Dermot McNamara, and Farrell Pelly. Robards and Eric Portman lived in the same building. Robards thinks "*A Touch of the Poet* is the best play O'Neill ever wrote, a fabulous play." The filming schedule in New York coincided with the five weeks *A Moon for the Misbegotten* was to play on Broadway. (Quintero directed Robards, Colleen Dewhurst, and Ed Flanders in a critically acclaimed production which established the play as another O'Neill masterpiece.) Robards began to rehearse Con Melody by day and play Jamie Tyrone by night, but quickly acknowledged the impossibility of the task. He withdrew from the project and Quintero quickly followed suit.

Not until 1977 did Quintero again contract to direct Robards in *A Touch of the Poet*, this time for producer Elliot Martin. Writer and O'Neill biographer Barbara Gelb attempted to pin down the methods by which Quintero had directed Robards for a quarter of a century:

"Jason and I understood each other, right away," Quintero says recalling the first time he directed Robards at Circle in the Square... "There was an open corridor between us, with no obstructions. There was never a feeling that I had to be careful, you know, not to say that. It has always been like that, also with Colleen and Gerry Page. They don't have to hear what I say, they sense what I feel. That's my kind of actor and I'm their kind of director."[4]

"I don't remember José actually telling me anything," Robards says, confirming this, at the end of the third week of rehearsal, "he's *acting* with us."[5] Gelb then contrasted the impact a director makes on a self-sufficient actor like George C. Scott and his impact on Robards who "develops a role slowly and emotionally, from within. Robards welcomes Quintero's suggestions and support—which is not to say that he is not a highly innovative actor. The collaboration between the two is far more typical of Quintero's directorial approach than is the intellectual and minimal collaboration between him and Scott."[6] Quintero told Barbara Gelb that he invoked a series of images to get Robards started:

> All the examples I give to Jason are emotional ones. For instance, I've talked to him about how it felt to Melody to live in the past, how his life has no meaning in the present. Who is Melody without his dreams? I think he is on the verge of madness when the play begins, like Hickey in *The Iceman Cometh*. And we talk about Mr. O'Neill. What must those years have been like when he was forgotten and could no longer write? He must have said to himself, "I was given the Nobel Prize."[7]

In putting the play on its feet, Quintero took O'Neill's stage directions selectively, according to Barbara Gelb. "He explained that O'Neill's stage directions—elaborate and fanciful and often quite impossible—are not, in his opinion, meant to be taken literally. They are, rather, meant as guides to characterization."[8] Nothing needed to be forced on Robards. Quintero explained:

> "If something doesn't become organic to Jason, we throw it out, but we're not afraid to try anything." One piece of business that became organic was the cold fury with which Robards, as Melody, crumpled a paper document whose contents he will not confront. Watching Robards in an early rehearsal, Quintero senses his wish to make the gesture—and his hesitation. Silently Quintero stepped up to Robards, ad-libbed the sense of his line and closed his fist around the piece of paper. "Once you set Jason on the right track…" Quintero leaves the sentence unfinished, but gestures to show that Robards will take flight. "Watch the way Jason deals with his cigar, as though it's the most deadly stiletto. His hand movements, his body movements are incredible." I will say things to him like, "try to catch the plume-like silhouette of Lord Byron." I never push him, because I know he is very daring. He was willing even to try taking out his bridge after his fight scene."[9]

Rehearsals focused on the complexity of Con Melody's character, locating the touch of the poet, throwing light on an avenue of approach the audience would need to reach Melody. For Robards, the title of the play refers not to Con, but to "the poet upstairs, that kid

Simon who is never seen. That's the touch of the poet." As Robards sees him:

> Con is reacting in opposition to the young generation growing up and to the society in which he's living. He's a rebel. To the Yanks like Deborah who come in, he's scum. He's angry and that's why he's still a drunk, because he never found out what it was that was eating him. It was wonderful for me to get a chance to play that kind of guy and know that underneath that he was something else. It's the mask that O'Neill puts into every play.

Robards is equivocal about Melody's military background: "Who knows what a hero of Talavara he was? I *read* all about Talavara. Christopher Plummer, who'd played Wellington, gave me a lot of stuff for research. I wanted to be familiar with the Peninsular Wars because I talk to Milo [Milo O'Shea, who played Jamie Cregan], about where we were on the map so I looked up that particular battle, but maybe it's all bullshit." This is an unusual choice, or nonchoice. Whether or not Melody distinguished himself at Talavara and was decorated by Wellington would seem to be the very spine of building Melody's character. The active choice would be to make him a fighting Irish devil who showed the English how it should be done.

Dermot McNamara [who played Paddy O'Dowd in the 1958 production, as well as the 1977-78 Quintero version, recalled] how, as the character of Con Melody developed, Con dwelt on his military and sexual prowess:

> Early in the play, Eric Portman was perfect when Con is being the British guy, a British officer immaculate on parade. He looked good. Maybe in the first act Jason who is all–American was not as happy in that cravat as he was later when he falls apart because then he was off to the races. I don't think Portman could have touched that and remained lucid. Robards has all that balls going for him all the time, no matter what he's playing. You can't dislike the man, you've got to feel what he feels. It's so powerful.

According to McNamara, Quintero built up Con's bravado until Mrs. Harford rejected his advances in the second act:

> That sets him off, in José's opinion, because he was a good-looking bloke and he had his way with women a lot. He was a major after all, with the uniform. He says, "A kiss will not be out of place now, my

dear," and she walks away from him. That killed him, that rejection, only that. He wasn't trying to get her in the sack at that moment, but imagine a man of his vanity and ego and Irishness, with a basic inferiority and the class distinction.

Barry Snider (Mickey Maloy) stressed the difficulty of locating the nature of the poet in Con:

> That was the center of the problem of the production. As he was described by José, he was a soldier, he was the hero of Talavara, he was that as a young man. The problem came in with the concept of the "poet," in his conception of himself as a poet, because he tended to have a kind of elitist attitude which those who are rather insecure feel and express, and he expressed it in such a way that Jason would go through the lines "I have not loved the world" and he would say, "I feel phony, phony saying that when I get out on the stage. Pretentious." The difficulty is, of course, in finding a way to say that the man is pretentious, because you can't say that he isn't. And Jason's instincts about that have got to be totally right. Jason is so unpretentious himself and he cuts through that sort of thing and he can see it a mile away. The hard part for an actor like Jason, who is so opposed to anything pretentious on stage, was to find some way to make this man, underneath all that, display some value. And he did, of course, find value in it in the transition, after he got drunk, from there on he was gorgeous. Those early scenes were the difficult part.

Snider examined the manner in which he thought Robards tried to create a poetic nature:

> If he were to ascribe a poetic nature to a character he would find a real poetic nature—that's not the sort of thing that Jason can play. He says, "that's bullshit." He would say that directly. The first part of the play— it's a problem with the play—you can do it as some actors do it, stand up straight and deliver it like that, you're a poet. Well, what does that mean? My impression of Jason was that he never felt totally satisfied with it. It's a problem with that man going on and on about what a poet he is. It's very difficult to solve.

Robards felt that Quintero's direction was "the clearest and hardest work he ever did. I've never seen him stick with a play like that. The great care that José put into the show, the preparation and the follow-up, all the way through the road to New York, paid off as the play went on." By and large the critics agreed. Marilyn Stasio's rave was the only review that implied that Quintero had succeeded by directing against the text:

> The character of Con is usually interpreted as O'Neill probably intended, as an irascible bull of a man very much like James O'Neill, a man whose bursts of cruelty can be forgiven because he has a speck of the artist's imagination. A touch of O'Neill if you will. Robards has the guts to defy this romantic excuse and to interpret Con's "gift" as a touch of the Devil. For all the charm and dignity he allows Con, Robards never glosses over the rough, even savage cruelty of the man.[10]

Most of the reviews, like the production itself, sought to locate just what constitutes the implications of the title. Wherein lies the touch of the poet? They focused, inevitably, on Robards' performance as Con.

Both *Newsweek* and *Time* were lavish in their praise of Robards. Jack Kroll wrote that "this is the poetry of crack-up and Jason Robards is the master actor of crack-up…. Some of his acting earlier in the play … is somewhat mannered and fussy."[11] Ted Kalem wrote that "to the role of Con Melody, Robards brings the deep-set, brooding eyes of profound melancholy, the harsh self-lacerating laugh that masks inner pain, the actorish stance of assuming, while mocking, the grand manner, the human love that becomes inhuman cruelty under the distillation of alcohol."[12] Kalem put his finger on, and accepted, "the actorish stance of assuming, while mocking, the grand manner." Other reviewers would not accept it.

Robards' military bearing was brought into question. John Simon wrote that "one does not believe in his military prowess or in his determined rise to specious respectability."[13] Michael Feingold wrote that "the body, even at maximum hauteur, does not have the force needed for a major of dragoons: the voice long ago settled into a permanent rasp and is short of sounding brass."[14]

Accents proved to be a problem. Mitch Erickson (stage manager) said that "José's strong suit is not dialect or speech of any kind, so he's not inclined to steer people in that direction." Milo O'Shea, Geraldine Fitzgerald (Nora Melody), and Dermot McNamara were all Irish-born and used their own accent. Robards had a much more complicated task. As Leonard Harris wrote, "Robards, an American, must play an Irishman trying to sound like an upperclass Englishman. It's not quite there."[15] Martin Gottfried wrote that "Robards is surely the great

O'Neill actor of our time, but when he tries a high British accent, he is an actor with a hot potato in his mouth."[16]

Beyond the technique of military bearing and English accent lay the ability to examine and project the cruel disparity between Con's military and social background in both Ireland and England and his present existence as a barkeeper. Producer Elliot Martin articulated the production's concept of Con Melody:

> The concept behind the work that Jason did on *Poet* was that this man was a bog–Irishman. That was his basic background, and he had been sent to an English academy to learn a certain amount of polish, but he never learned it. He was a tough, gutter Irishman. Rather than playing him from the other point of view, which was to cast it as an Englishman who was terribly grand and try to play the rough bog–Irishman. In our discussions, we justified it the other way around. There was a lot of baggy pants in that character, basically. When he became grand, it was phony grand. After all, he was in a run-down, early American tavern which was very Irish-oriented and if anybody put on airs—if you go to Ireland today and put on airs, they'd throw you right out. Our point of view was that Jason was very right because he's a bog–Irishman.

Stage manager Mitch Erickson agreed: "What with Jason and his wry view of life and his sense of humor, I don't remember any attempt to make Con a great figure or person. He wasn't a great man fallen, but a man with great aspirations who was living a huge lie and gets his comeuppance."

Every critic granted Robards the grandeur of his final twenty minutes in the role, when he is beaten and humiliated, but six major critics/publications found the pivotal element of the production (as articulated by Martin and played by Robards) either misconceived or badly executed. Harold Clurman, who had directed the 1958 production, wrote:

> What Robards cannot convincingly achieve is personal grandeur. I am not sure that José Quintero as director has wholly understood the play. For while Melody is something of a fool in his Byronic swagger, his aspiration to and feeling for nobility are real. He is a dreamer, not a faker; his whole being yearns for what was sound and forever worthy in the old aristocratic ideal of the English gentry, an ideal O'Neill held in high esteem.... Melody's downfall at the hands of the wealthy New England "tradesmen" is pathetic and meaningful to the play only if we discern the idealistic truth hidden beneath his boastful postures

and lordly behavior. There can be no real pathos in the crackup of a pipsqueak or a phony.[17]

Dean Valentine wrote of Robards:

He plays Melody as a foppish buffoon. Descending the stairs caparisoned in his major's uniform, he looks merely like a poseur, a man too small for his britches; certainly he has not the trace of a hero of the Battle of Talavara, the classy soldier decorated by Wellington. He crumples up his fingers, rolls his eyelids to denote a touch of the demoniac, curls his lip and sticks out his tongue. These gestures, it is true, frequently produce the desired effect; a con man whose lies and sarcasm overlay an infinite pool of disgust with the world. The desired effect, though, is not the right one, and it is difficult not to feel that Robards is hamming it up at the cost of a truly heroic Melody.[18]

Elliot Norton wrote:

It is, of course, true that Melody is in both cases mimicking manners and accents which are not quite his own. Although he was born in a shanty, he was educated in an English school, and elevated to the rank of major in a prestigious English regiment. He would have more style and authority, even if these are faded, and a much less fraudulent manner of speech than that of Jason Robards. The major is, in a sense, a phony. But not so desperately ridiculous, so amateurishly imitative, as Jason Robards makes him.[19]

Richard Eder, Stanley Kauffmann, and Walter Kerr all focused their reservations about Robards' Melody on the crucial seduction scene. Eder wrote, "Mr. Robards acts too old. With marvelous timing and control, changing courses as suddenly as a waterbug, he spectacularly manages Melody's silky deviousness, his aristocratic airs, but his delusion is something he mostly toys with. He may get angry asserting it but it is a testy anger.... Mr. Robards' semi-seduction is all style and buffoonery."[20]

After commending Robards' final 20 minutes, Stanley Kauffmann went on to say:

But in the major part of the role (pun intended), he is, frankly, appalling. I could hardly believe what I was seeing and hearing. Instead of a Byron-quoting ex-officer, a fallen emperor with a ragged retinue, we get mugging and caricature. For just one instance: when the elegant Mrs. Harford, Simon's mother, enters unannounced, Robards turns from his mirror and discovers her. Then he does a full unabashed "take" from her face to the audience, like a baggy-pants comic when a pretty girl comes in. Throughout, until the very end, he kept reminding me of Harvey Korman of "The Carol Burnett Show" playing a lord. Then I realized what was happening. Robards (and his director) took the "elevated" portion of the role as impersonation, a kind of W. C. Fields act of grandeur. Nothing could be falser or most destructive of the play. Either the grand Con is *not* "acting" or there is no tragedy. The two actors I've seen previously in the part, Eric Portman and Denholm Elliott, had their shortcomings, but both of them understood that basic truth. Without it, without Con's belief in himself as a gentleman, all we get is the exposure of a self-conscious faker which is trivial.[21]

As soon as Elliot Martin was reminded that Kauffmann had referred to Melody as "a fallen emperor with a ragged retinue," Martin burst out triumphantly, "You see! *That's* miscasting. That's *really* miscasting, because this character was a low-born Irishman whose father, somehow or other, scraped together the money and pulled enough strings to get him into an English school where they probably made terrible fun of him. So, for the rest of his life, he'd send them up if he got the chance."

Walter Kerr concluded:

If all this is to hold up in the theater the poetic impulse must be constantly present and be recognized for what it is. Those who cling to it may be fools but they must be ambiguously fools: men with a trace of actual talent, men with color on their tongue, men of ludicrously thwarted aspiration. And it is here that the present production collapses completely. Until the satisfyingly vigorous final scene, neither Mr. Quintero nor Mr. Robards suggests that there is anything to be salvaged from a fantasist's inventive brain, from a memory of heroism on the battlefield under Wellington, from an ostentatious fondness for Byron's rhythms, for, if you will, an unquenchable thirst for blarney.

Mr. Robards looks right when he enters, straightbacked in a black frock coat, lace at his throat and wrists. Almost at once, however, he is reduced to an idle popinjay, tyrant to no purpose. Nervously and noisily rattling a whiskey bottle against a glass for his first sip of the morning, he is very nearly a cartoon. The one-dimensional humbuggery continues as he wriggles his fingers high in the air like a barnstorming

Osric, as he turns from self-adulation in a mirror to hike his eyebrows at the audience in a vaudeville leer, as he adopts stances that constantly seem to be inviting someone to slap him across the face with a glove. "Thank God," he purrs, "I still bear the stamp of an officer and a gentleman." But he doesn't really; he bears the stamp of a fop. When he proposes to flatter the visiting Miss Miller by pawing her, the clumsiness of the gesture may be half-right. But surely it should have another half to it; some echo of the suave gallantry that must have been his as a young man.[22]

In his review of *A Moon for the Misbegotten*, Stanley Kauffmann wrote of Robards' performance that "essentially this is the fourth installment of Robards' performance of the O'Neill character; it's virtually the same man he played in *The Iceman Cometh*, *Hughie* and, of course, *Long Day's Journey Into Night*. Robards does it superbly. It's the only character I've ever seen him do superbly."[23] In his review of *A Touch of the Poet*, Kauffmann emphasizes the difference between Con Melody and the other O'Neill characters Robards had played: "In the last 20 minutes or so of the play, Jason Robards is fine as Melody, on the other side of the catastrophe in which Con is degraded. When the role comes *to* Robards, when he can once again do the one character he can do well—the ironic, self-loathing drunk, the Jamie of *Long Day's Journey* and *A Moon for the Misbegotten*—he fulfills it."[24]

To take Kauffmann one step further, the four O'Neill roles Robards has played are all based heavily on James O'Neill Jr., whereas Con is based on James O'Neill Sr., and set 100 years earlier than the Jamie characters. Robards is certainly no stranger to fatherhood or to the military. With his extended family and his experiences in the Pacific during World War II, Robards has all the life experience needed to play Melody. Until 1977, when he played Melody, Robards' career, certainly his great successes, consisted largely of sons rebelling against the imposition of the parental will. It is a very specific acting impulse. Even if the parental figure does not appear on stage, the son is still able to lash out at restraints. In *A Touch of the Poet*, however, as domestic drama, it is Con the father who imposes the restraints, who behaves arbitrarily, who sets the tone. It is a totally different acting impulse and Robards did not seem to be at home with it.

Robards, understandably, rejected this theory and refused to be pigeonholed: "This is a gift I've got and I don't know anything about that gift. I'm just lucky that I've got it, that I've got *some* of it. It's rubbed off on me, from my dad or wherever it came from, my genes or my experience, but I don't question it. I don't start tearing it apart because then you end up in a Strasberg class and, Jesus, who wants to be there?"

A Touch of the Poet is not often produced, but there has been a striking consistency in trying to capture the essence of Con. In 1947, the Theatre Guild wished to cast either Spencer Tracy or Laurence Olivier. Thirty years later, producer Elliot Martin said that Con "was a tough, gutter Irishman." Until the 1977–78 *Poet*, Con had been played twice in New York City by Eric Portman and Denholm Elliott, two terribly grand (and gifted) Englishmen. Robards was the first American playing the role and he made some passive acting choices: the touch of the poet resides in an offstage character and Con may or may not have been decorated by Wellington. That's a lot to give up. It pleased some of the critics. Ted Kalem, for instance, believed that Con is "as confirmed a dream addict as any of the tosspots in *The Iceman Cometh*."[25] From the six demurring critics included here, for whom the touch of the poet is *definitely* in Con himself who was *definitely* honored by Wellington, Robards was bound to take a hammering.

The production remains one of Robards' fondest achievements: "I kept learning doing that play daily, every day, until it closed nine months after we'd started. I was always learning something as an actor. I was soaring. It was like finding a new color to put on the canvas every day. It was so exciting to go to the theater to do that play."

NOTES

1. Arthur and Barbara Gelb, *O'Neill* (New York: Harper and Row, 1962), 884–85.

2. Louis Sheaffer, *O'Neill: Son and Artist* (Boston: Little, Brown, 1973), 576.

3. Lawrence Langner, *The Magic Curtain* (New York: Dutton, 1951), 409.

4. Barbara Gelb, "A Touch of the Tragic," *The New York Times Magazine* (11 Dec., 1977), 126.

5. B. Gelb, 126.

6. B. Gelb, 126.

7. B. Gelb, 127.

8. B. Gelb, 127.

9. B. Gelb, 127.

10. Marilyn Stasio, *Cue* (20 Feb. 1978), 20.

11. Jack Kroll, "Symphony of Despair," *Newsweek* (9 Jan. 1978), 71.

12. Ted E. Kalem, "Dream Addict," *Time* (9 Jan 1978), 68.

13. John Simon, "A Touch Is Better Than None," *New York* (16 Jan. 1978), 57.

14. Michael Feingold, "O'Neill's Way," *The Village Voice* (19 Jan. 1978), 67.

15. Leonard Harris, "An American Chronicle," *SoHo Weekly News* (12 Jan. 1978), 40.

16. Martin Gottfried, "Cult of the Second Rate," *Saturday Review* (4 Mar. 1978), 41.

17. Harold Clurman, rev. of *A Touch of the Poet, Nation* (21 Jan. 1978), 60–61.

18. Dean Valentine, "Blarney and Bluster," *New Leader* (30 Jan. 1978), 25.

19. Eliot Norton, "Robards Falters in *Touch of the Poet*," Boston *Herald American*, (2 Jan. 1978), 30

20. Richard Eder, "*A Touch of the Poet* Staged by Quintero on Broadway," *New York Times* (29 Dec. 1977), B, 13.

21. Stanley Kauffmann, rev. of *A Touch of the Poet, New Republic* (28 Jan. 1978), 24–25.

22. Walter Kerr, "Vintage O'Neill—But with the Critical Ambiguity Missing," *New York Times* (8 Jan. 1978), D 5.

23. Kauffmann, rev. of *A Moon for the Misbegotten, New Republic* (26 Jan. 1974), 34.

24. Kauffmann, rev. of *A Touch of the Poet*, 24–25.

25. Kalem, 68.

Recreating a Myth: The Iceman Cometh in Washington, D.C., 1985

by Sheila Hickey Garvey

> The following is reprinted from *The Eugene O'Neill Review*, vol. 9, 1, Winter 1985, 17–23, by permission of the *Review* and its editor, Frederick Wilkins. Four new paragraphs were added to the end.

Unnoticed by the audience, José Quintero left during the third act of *The Iceman Cometh*'s Saturday night opening and quietly conferred with an associate in a corner of the Kennedy Center's lobby. He looked tired, burdened, his tall robust frame hunched over with concern. At the Tuesday preview he had seemed more confident and relaxed and had used the play's three intermissions to meditate while strolling outdoors on the Center's Potomac promenade where the river's breeze was comforting and soothed him as he considered the remaining brushstrokes to apply while completing the pictorial canvas of O'Neill's playwriting masterpiece. Saturday night, however, his work was completed. The forces which had compelled him to take on O'Neill's purgatory of tortured souls had once again been met. Undistracted, he could now feel the weight of the week's pressure.

Ironically, the opening of *The Iceman Cometh* almost thirty years before had been easier because there were no myths to be challenged. In 1956, O'Neill was considered a has-been and Quintero's reputation as the definitive director of O'Neill's works was yet to be established. In the fifties, Quintero could still drink his anxieties away safely. The maelstrom years of his alcoholism were ahead of him. His successful struggle with recovery and sobriety was unimaginable.

On that August evening in 1985, Quintero met the awesome task sober. Night after night he had sat watching a barroom full of dere-licts happily drowning their memories and had survived. In redoing *The Iceman Cometh*, Quintero had chosen to place personal as well as professional demands on himself. He was not just reweaving a historic production; he was working with material that placed incessant pres-sure on his subconscious obsession. Quintero's conscious focus, how-ever, was not on his alcoholism: it was on the awesome task of attempting to recreate an American theatrical myth.

Quintero has been evading queries regarding his interpretation of *Iceman* in the current production, fearing the inevitable comparisons which would be made to the legendary original. The Washington reviews have been rapturous, insuring the show's transfer to New York when it closes on September 14th. Quintero looks upon this initial success with caution. The critical climate in Washington could be mercurial, a deceptive calm before a potential tempest. Although he has directed many celebrated O'Neill revivals (*A Touch of the Poet, A Moon for the Misbegotten, Hughie*), he is well aware that in New York he will face an audience with expectations deeply influenced by his past success with the same play. New York's recollections of the 1956 *Iceman* is vivid.

Quintero is not the only one connected with ANT's *Iceman* who is haunted with memories of the Circle in the Square production. The current work brings together many of the original artists who made the Circle's production so remarkable. Jason Robards recreates the character of Theodore Hickman (Hickey), the role which catapulted his acting career. Actor James Greene reappears as the mournful Jimmy tomorrow. Roger Stevens, artistic director of the Kennedy Center and one of the original production's backers, is the reason why the 1985 production is being sheltered by ANT.

On the day the unanimously favorable Washington reviews came out, Jason Robards and James Greene were in the Kennedy Center's green room candidly reminiscing with me about the 1956 production. As the interview began, Peter Sellars, artistic director of ANT, passed Robards on his way backstage. He spotted Robards and called out,

Sellars. Hi, Maestro. Congratulations please. (Laughter.)

Robards. How are you?

Sellars. Great.

Robards. I only saw one ummmm thing.

Sellars. Oh, well, the rest are just head over heels.

Robards. See, I figured I'd better not read any more.

Sellars. They can't help themselves. (Laughter.)

Sellars' distinctive cackle trails him as he disappears down the hall. Robards and Greene are obviously spurred by the critics' positive response and are more than delighted to talk. The two men are friends of long standing who first met at the Circle in the Square while performing there in a Quintero-directed production of *American Gothic*. Robards begins the dialogue by affectionately recalling that it was Greene who had told him that Quintero was staging a revival of the 1946 Broadway failure, *The Iceman Cometh*: "We were all struggling actors and we all used to talk about who was doing what so we could go up and see about a job ... making the rounds." Greene had just returned from an audition at the Circle. Knowing that Robards was "between engagements," Greene insisted that he "get right over there and let José know you're available."

Quintero was interested in using Robards in the role of Willie Oban, the alcoholic lawyer; but Robards wanted to play the pivotal character of Hickey. He had seen the 1946 production and believed he could play the role. Quintero thought Robards was too young for the part but allowed him to give a reading of Hickey's fourth-act monologue. Robards already had it memorized. He gave an audition that stunned Quintero. Robards was Hickey. Quintero took a chance and gave Robards the role despite the age discrepancy. It was a gamble that paid off. The critics were beside themselves with accolades for Robards' portrayal. Even today, Robards and Hickey are synonymous.

Robards' and Greene's remembrances moved to recollections of the old Circle in the Square and its comfortable "club-like" atmosphere. In 1956, the Circle—now located at Broadway and 50th Street—was on Sheridan Square in Greenwich Village. The building it occupied was a former nightclub converted into an arena theatre. Performances at the "old Circle" took place on the club's former dance floor. Audience members would pass an aged oak bar to be seated at tiny cloth-covered tables. The first Circle in the Square was the catalyst for the Off Broadway movement. Its reputation for producing landmark revivals was interwoven with the mystique of an atmospheric and intimate performance space.

Both Greene and Robards were well aware of the pitfalls of the old Circle's aura when beginning rehearsals for the ANT production of *Iceman*. Greene recalls having great qualms. "I was so worried about doing this play on a proscenium stage. You just thought, 'it's not going to have the same feeling....'" Robards nodded while listening intently to Greene's comments. Finishing Greene's thoughts, Robards confessed to having trouble shaking the belief that "part of the success of doing *Iceman* back in '56 was doing it at the Circle. That theatre was the perfect space."

Ben Edwards had created a set for the ANT production which differed significantly from David Hays' 1956 single-room setting. Edwards saw the play as needing two distinct playing areas: the bar would be on a revolve and would disappear when scenes occurred in the saloon's back room. During rehearsal, however, Quintero decided that Edwards' idea didn't work. In Quintero's perception the play's developing conflict hinged on the relentless and claustrophobic presence of the emotionally frozen characters. After several pressured meetings a new approach was forged.

Revising the set mid-way through the production's rehearsal period was a major risk. Time was of the essence with the Washington opening looming, but to Robards and Greene the new floor plan revealed familiar home territory. Edwards' new ground plan for a unit set was similar in concept to the 1956 production. A slight angle in the bar-side wall would suggest the division between both rooms. Shifts in focus between the bar and backroom would be established by subtle changes in the lighting and the stillness of non-speaking characters.

Robards' intuition is that Quintero aimed Edwards toward the recreation of an arena effect on the Eisenhower Theatre's proscenium stage. "José had a thing with that circular apron, a sort of sweep, a sort of round feeling that he wanted to establish. Don't you find, Jimmy?" Greene concurs: "In 1956 we had an audience sitting around three sides. The way the tables are set up now is very similar to the way they were at the Circle. The physical relationship between the characters is duplicated. The bar seems to be in the same place. Harry is to my right. Joe Mott, the Captain and the General are to my left. It's amazing. I feel as if I'm in the same production."

Robards believes that, despite the fact that they are now playing on a proscenium stage with a much larger house, "The feeling in the room is the same. Maybe it's an unconscious thing. Maybe you project if you are trying to get the message across. You do it without thinking. But the intensity is the same if you believe in the words. You're right, Jimmy. It's just as intimate here as it was at the old Circle. I can feel those silences and the audience breathing."

Robards' and Greene's interpretation of Quintero's concept for the current *Iceman* is revealing. Their dialogue contradicts many of the Washington preview articles which portrayed Quintero as having little recollection of his original staging. In the *Washington Times*, Quintero is quoted as telling reporter Hap Erstein that "the play has become a totally new experience. I found that I remember very, very little—as much as I remember of myself 30 years ago." It is apparent that Quintero is sending up smoke-screen messages for self protection. He wants the ANT production perceived as a "new" work. Perhaps it is recollections of the critics' response to the opening performance of the 1956 *Iceman* which causes Quintero to be evasive.

As Greene describes it: "There was something electric about that day. It's easy to say now when you know you made history, but it was a particularly exciting theatrical experience. It was an opening matinee because the critics had deadlines to get their reviews in on time, with the length of the play (four and a half hours). We had played the first three acts and were coming back to take our places for Act Four in dim light. The audience burst into applause, and it was … spontaneous, not just a few people here and there applauding and the rest picking it up. They sensed that the actors were coming back and, with a whole act to go, they were just that moved and excited by the first three acts of the play that they were honoring us even before the play was over. Jason hadn't even done his aria yet. Peter Falk, who was playing Rocky the bartender, turned to Jason and said, 'don't blow it now, Jason.'"

Such retrospection shows why the ties which bind this particular play to the Circle in the Square are multi-woven. Quintero was a founder and former producer of the Circle. Unfortunately, discussing aspects of his years with that theatre is painful because they are bound up with his years of alcoholism. Quintero is quoted as telling Erstein, "I remember bits and pieces of myself and see myself running up and down the Circle, but I don't remember much else." Yet the same theatre enabled him to hone his directing technique because he was able to work there regularly. Quintero's time at the Circle between 1951 and 1963 solidified his reputation as one of the great directors of his generation. Still, Quintero's mastery had not been fully realized until the 1956 *Iceman* revival. The religious scope and broad thematic landscape of O'Neill's late masterwork touched Quintero almost mystically. The O'Neill play offered the challenge of orchestrating clashing themes sung out by endearing, yet tortured characters, most of whom were alcoholic. Because Quintero shared the same agony, he well understood the characters' anguish and spiritual conflict. O'Neill's stylistic and self-conscious mix of expressionism and realism perfectly suited Quintero's directorial approach, which was deeply personal and idiosyncratic.

Robards relishes describing Quintero's directing and notes ways he leaves his signature on the current production: "José's staging is very formal in a strange way. It's very stylized. Characters stop and listen to each other and don't move when the other guy is talking. José does all the good things that are missing in today's theatre. The production's not fast-paced or busy. It's clear. José said, 'it's got to be clean, clear. I don't want a lot of extraneous motion.' It's hard to keep a big company like that together."

Greene elaborates: "It's particularly tricky after Hickey's final Act Four exit because we're coming out of our stupor. We're starting to party again, yet we are constantly interrupted by what is happening stage-left between Larry and Parritt. We have to wait each time they have an exchange. Then we go back to moments of joviality to be interrupted again. It's impossible to do it totally naturalistically and there's no reason that it should be done that way."

Greene muses about the fact that Quintero has refused to cut the play, noting that the 1946 Broadway premiere failed because O'Neill's script was so severely pruned: José is just as interested in the silences in a play as he is in the dialogue. He thinks that there is life there on stage and life within a play even when somebody isn't speaking. And he has the courage to just slow down with everything. Very few directors would take the time that José allows the actors to take in Act One.

Both Robards and Greene concur that the ANT version recreates many of the visual images Quintero had used in the 1956 production. Robards recalls that Quintero had had "that serpentine table" arranged in the same manner. The Washington critics called it "the Last Supper," but Greene denies that Quintero's intentions were overtly religious: "I don't think José ever thought about the last supper." Robards agrees: "No, no, never. Nor the Pieta when Colleen and I did *A Moon for the Misbegotten*. José says he never thought of it. Everybody said, 'look at this. José said, 'They're reading all this stuff into it ... me, a failed Catholic.'"

Robards warms to the subject of symbolism and relates what he calls "the religious vein" apparent in Quintero's work to O'Neill's depiction of Hickey. Because he is the son of a "preacher, a salvationist," and is also a salesman, Robards thinks Hickey's approach to life is colored with religious motives. He notes that Hickey uses phrases such as "brother and sister" when speaking with his barroom cronies. In referring to Hickey's manner, the characters say, "listen to him whoopin' up all that hell fire." Robards concludes that the religious imagery is inherent in the text and that Quintero is simply responding to what is already present: "José doesn't feel those things consciously. But, in a way, I suppose we've thought of all these things."

Discussion about artistic intentions triggers a memory in Robards, who suddenly exclaims, "What is it about this play? It's something Peter [Sellars] said the other night which I'd never thought about. Is this play subconsciously or unconsciously about alcoholism? What do you think?" Greene is surprised: "I never thought so." "I agree," says Robards. "But Peter thinks this is a play about alcohol. Now he wants to do plays about all of the American problems. Next season he wants to do a play about abortion, then he wants to do a play about suicide. But I don't know. That's why I mentioned it. I felt very funny the other night when he brought the subject up. I don't know if he believes it.

But I've been thinking about it since then. I've been thinking about it my whole day off."

Settling the issue seems crucial to Robards' peace of mind. Quintero had not been alone in his alcoholism; Robards was once violently ill from the same addiction, and Greene had witnessed the worst of their drinking. Quintero's health was ravaged from alcohol abuse; Robards almost died in an alcohol-related automobile accident. Some ten years ago Quintero and Robards fought and won the battle to stay sober. Since that time they have publicly discussed their problem.

In the hopes of preventing others from suffering the same torment, Robards has been working with alcoholics through a recovery program at the Mayo Clinic. He appears there regularly to discuss his fight with alcohol. Because the character of Hickey is also alcoholic, Robards often uses Hickey's fourth-act monologue to demonstrate two signs of alcoholism, enablement and denial. The piece shows that Hickey's wife Evelyn encourages his drinking by continuing to forgive his behavior. The result is that Hickey, who already despises himself for his weakness, begins to hate his wife.

But Robards doesn't want the public's knowledge of his addiction to overshadow the significance of the *Iceman* event. He looks to Greene for help in articulating his conflict: "When Peter brought the whole subject up, I thought, I don't play the monologue that way when I'm performing. I never think of it as a teaching tool when I'm doing *Iceman*. When you have to go out alone and begin it, then it's a teaching tool. This play isn't about alcohol. Is it about alcohol? I always thought the play was about dreams and reality. I don't want to make that statement. Is O'Neill making that statement?"

Greene considers Robards' reasoning: "Only the sober people die. You and Parritt." Robards appears pained: "Is that what O'Neill's saying? You've got to be drunk to live: Is that it?"

They begin to reconsider the play, noting the ramifications of seeing it as a single-issue piece. Greene, who is not an alcoholic, tries to reassure Robards, saying he believes there are many ideas and issues in the play which place O'Neill's work on a grander, broader scale. After considering Greene's comments, Robards begins to relax. The conversation then turns to the more immediate implications of *Iceman*'s coming transfer to New York. When Robards leaves to attend an appointment, the conversation with Greene continues.

James Greene summarizes the importance of Iceman's arrival when he describes Jason Robards' first entrance as Hickey: "One of the things that I love about Jason's performance is that in a very short time he shows you the old Hickey. You see that. It only lasts for a short time, about five minutes. But in those five minutes when he comes through the door, it's Santa Claus. It's so theatrical, so wonderful. And, when you're on stage for that hour, waiting for him, and when he comes through the door, it's a joy, truly a joy. And of course, Jason always does a different song every night and we all look forward to that. It's a wonderful theatrical moment for an actor just to remember that. It's like extraordinary. In five minutes you see exactly what it was like when Hickey used to come there and get drunk, and they'd all get drunk and he'd tell awful jokes and they'd sing. And then the play twists so quickly and you never see it again for the rest of the play. But in those first five minutes you know why the characters loved him so and looked forward to having him come for Harry's birthday."

When it opened in New York on September 29, 1985, the Quintero/Robards revival of Iceman was showered with praise. Two radio reviewers described it as "spellbinding" (Alvin Klein on WNYC) and "shimmering" (Jeffrey Lyons on WCBS). Clive Barnes, writing in the *New York Post* (30 September 1985), declared it a production which brought "distinction" to the entire theatre season. When *The Iceman Cometh* transferred from Washington to the Lunt-Fontanne Theatre on Broadway, it played for a scheduled twelve-week limited engagement. *Iceman* received four 1986 Tony Award nominations for Best Reproduction, Best Director, Best Scenic Designer (Ben Edwards) and Best Lighting (Thomas R. Skelton).

For José Quintero, this newer version of *The Iceman Cometh* signified another landmark O'Neill triumph. For his direction of the 1985 revival of *The Iceman Cometh* and in recognition for his outstanding career as the preeminent director of the plays of Eugene O'Neill, José Quintero was honored with elevation to the Theatre Hall of Fame.

For Jason Robards, the tackling of Hickey in such high profile venues Off- and On-Broadway in both his youth and in his maturity was precedent setting. In doing so, Robards set a standard for American actors to use O'Neill, to hone their craft in the same manner British actors use Shakespeare or Russian actors use Chekhov. The stature of the achievement for the American Theatre was undeniable.

This joint O'Neill collaboration between Quintero and Robards reaffirmed, once again, their right to be regarded as the foremost interpreters of the plays of Eugene O'Neill.

Jason Robards:
Crunching the Numbers

by Madeline Smith and Richard Eaton

Madeline Smith is Professor of English, California University
of Pennsylvania; Richard Eaton is Professor of English, West
Virginia University, and editor of *The Eugene O'Neill Society
Newsletter*. They recently published *Eugene O'Neill: An Annotated International Bibliography, 1973 through 1999* (McFarland,
2001).

We are theater-goers and bibliographers for whom Jason Robards
held up the mirror to O'Neill. Over the years we had been captivated
by his performances in *A Moon for the Misbegotten, Long Day's Journey
Into Night, Hughie,* and *A Touch of the Poet*. We attended the 1992 meeting of the Eugene O'Neill Society at the MLA convention in New
York when Robards reminisced about his experiences reading and acting in plays by O'Neill. We recall his performance in *Misbegotten*
which, for us, will always be *the* performance. Like most O'Neillians,
we agree, subjectively, that Robards did more than any other actor to
reinvigorate the playwright's reputation. Our tribute to Robards' memory will be a survey of performances and reviews to see if our subjective assumption can be proven as historically factual. Did the lightning
of his performances spark imitations of his success in the same and

other O'Neill plays? Did Robards' performances inspire more critical and scholarly responses than others' performances of the same plays had previously spawned? Were the plays suddenly and subsequently translated into other languages? We knew we risked the logical fallacy of post hoc, ergo propter hoc; still we thought, for Jason Robards' sake, we'd give it a try.

But before any of these questions can be addressed we should answer another question. Who (after the playwright himself, of course) had the most influence in creating the roles Jason Robards played? The director or the actor? Who deserves the credit for resurrecting O'Neill? Should we be here celebrating Quintero rather than Robards? Or perhaps some immeasurable combination of the two? Quintero suggests that Robards, like Byron, awoke one morning to find himself famous—because of Brooks Atkinson's review of *Iceman* (Quintero 117). Atkinson, we remember, describes Robards' Hickey as showing qualities that were new to the character (Atkinson, "Tragedy"). Quintero himself tells us that when Robards read for the role, he delivered the long fourth-act monologue, "arms stretched out, begging for the crucifixion. Rivers of sweat distorting all his features. But driving his points cleanly, with the precision and clarity of the mad, of the holy, of the devil." At that moment, Quintero knew who would play Hickey (169–70).

Edwin McDonough, years later, interviewed actor after actor in the cast of that same *Iceman*. He observed that almost invariably the actors claimed that they themselves developed their interpretations of their roles; apparently Quintero's contribution was to let the actors struggle/stumble towards their own characterizations and, then, step in to indicate approval when he sensed they had achieved their goal (McDonough, especially 40–45). Of course, a production is not just the actors. The two O'Neill plays Robards attempted without Quintero's direction (*Long Day's Journey* in 1976 and *Ah, Wilderness!* in 1988) received very muted responses, while the joint efforts of the actor and the director were always successful. Obviously, then, as we decided, it was "some immeasurable combination of the two"; but the evidence suggests that Jason made independent contributions as an actor. Surely it's the person on the front line, the actor, who has the edge.[1]

When José Quintero mounted his first O'Neill play, *The Iceman Cometh*, Robards got his crack at the role of Hickey, much to the chagrin of his agent, Archer King, who told the actor he was "out of his mind to go into a five-hour bomb by O'Neill ... and that nobody in his right mind was going to sit through all that shit" (McDonough 31). But, of course, time and Robards' talent proved King wrong; the production garnered raves for both Quintero's direction and Robards' interpretation of his role. Brooks Atkinson, in his review of the opening night performance, after crediting the director, turned his eye on Robards, who, the critic thought, played Hickey "as an evangelist. His unction, condescension and piety introduced an element of moral affectation that clarified that perspective of the drama as a whole. His heartiness, his aura of good fellowship, give the character of Hickey a feeling of evil mischief it did not have before" (Atkinson, "Tragedy"). Indeed, critical reception was generally so enthusiastic that the production continued for a 565-performance run (Gelb 20 and *Who's Who*, 15th ed., 1664).

While the reputation of the 1956 production is well established, its success is even more significant when compared with the original production ten years earlier and several other O'Neill plays staged in the intervening years. In 1946 *The Iceman Cometh* played in New York to very mixed reviews, and clearly did not "herald the long awaited New Age of O'Neill..." (Miller 71). The "mixed reviews" ranged from "action draggeth, dialogue reeketh, play stinketh," "longwinded," "blue pencil ... needed" to "first-rate," "magnificent," "absorbing, disturbing, magnificently acted" (as surveyed by Miller 343–49). Though the production lasted long enough to justify its going on the road, it was still thought to be a "botched production" (McDonough 23). In 1947 *A Moon for the Misbegotten*'s opening, out of town (Columbus, Ohio), was a "catastrophe" (Miller's word, 36). The play never made it to New York. *S. S. Glencairn* was attempted in 1948, but even the presence of José Ferrer (acting and producing) was insufficient to keep it alive beyond 14 performances. That same year there was a college production of *Lazarus Laughed*, at Fordham—dubbed "lukewarm." In 1951 an "*Anna Christie*" with Celeste Holm and Kevin McCarthy died despite its merits, after 29 performances (Atkinson, "*Anna*"). A 1952 *Desire Under the Elms*, staged by Harold Clurman, was able to hold on for only 46 performances, and that despite a "powerful" Karl Malden as Cabot. And the same year another attempt at *A Moon for the Misbegotten* was viewed as a *Desire Under the Elms* "grown old and hoary and randy" (McCarthy), while a new *Long Voyage Home* was virtually still-born at the Provincetown Playhouse.

There follows a lapse of four years with no major attempts at an O'Neill production.[2] Then comes the 1956 *Iceman* at the Circle in the Square, holding audiences for an astounding 565 performances. And opening that same year was the premiere of *Long Day's Journey Into Night* with 390 performances. The Hickey role in *Iceman* had to be recast so that Robards could play James Tyrone Jr. in *Journey*. In effect O'Neill, three years dead, had been reborn.

After 1956 hardly a year passes without a major, or at least strong, production of O'Neill. In 1957 we have *Moon for the Misbegotten* with Franchot Tone, Cyril Cusack and Wendy Hiller. The 1958 offering was *A Touch of the Poet* with Kim Stanley and Helen Hayes. In 1959 *The Great God Brown* was staged by the Phoenix Theatre, with Robert Lansing. The year 1961 saw *Diff'rent* and *Long Voyage Home* at the Mermaid. George C. Scott, Rip Torn, and Colleen Dewhurst, Quintero directing, did *Desire Under the Elms* for 164 performances in 1963. That same year Quintero also directed *Strange Interlude* with Franchot Tone, Ben Gazzara, Geraldine Page, Pat Hingle, and Jane Fonda. Then in 1964 we have a *Marco Millions*, with Hal Holbrook and David Wayne, and the American premiere of *Hughie* with Jason Robards again, both directed by Quintero.

In the last forty-five years, 1956 to the present, we see O'Neill on stage, with the likes of Harold Clurman, Theodore Mann, Arvin Brown, and Jonathan Miller directing, while on the marquees are Geraldine Fitzgerald, Katharine Hepburn, Charlton Heston, James Earl Jones, Stacy Keach, Jack Lemmon, John Lithgow, Lee Marvin, Liam Neeson, Laurence Olivier, Al Pacino, Anthony Quayle, Vanessa Redgrave, Natasha Richardson, Ralph Richardson, Robert Ryan, Daniel Travanti, Liv Ullmann, Sam Waterston, and Margaret Whiting. Only a sample but at the same time a roster of some of the most prominent actors—both film and stage—of the second half of the twentieth century, American, Irish, and English. It would probably be impossible to compute the number of O'Neill productions in English, since 1956, but we can document 569 produced between 1973 and 1999.[3]

Abroad within the five years after 1956, Robards plays O'Neill in Paris. *A Moon for the Misbegotten* premieres in London, as does *A Touch of the Poet*, which then goes to the Venice Festival. Quintero directs a *Moon for the Misbegotten* in Spoleto in 1958; *Long Day's Journey* plays at the Abbey in Dublin; and an Italian *Journey* premieres in Milan.

Iceman opens in London, and Quintero directs O'Neill for the Edinburgh Festival. *More Stately Mansions* and *Long Day's Journey* have Swedish productions in 1958 and 1962, respectively, and Quintero directs Liv Ullmann in *A Moon for the Misbegotten* in Norway. In the last quarter century, there have been Arabic, Belgian, Bulgarian, Chinese, Czechoslovakian, Dutch, French, German, Greek, Hungarian, Indian, Italian, Norwegian, Polish, Romanian, and Swedish productions of O'Neill (see Note 3). The Russians had translated eight O'Neill plays between 1925 and 1933. Thereafter there were no new translations until the "resurrection" when in the next decade there were five new translations (Fridshtein 84).[4]

The spate of O'Neill productions after 1956 is easy to document, but one might wonder whether the theatrical interest produced scholarship. There the evidence can be pretty difficult to assess. Inspired by performance, a scholar writes an essay or book. But how much time elapses between inspiration and when that essay or book is published? Europe gives us strong indications of an impact. Between 1946 and 1955, there were only five foreign-language items recorded in the most wide-ranging bibliography—in German, Italian, Norwegian. But for the next FIVE years, there are 51 items—in Danish, Dutch, Finnish, French, Icelandic, Polish, Spanish, and Swedish, as well as German, Italian, and Norwegian (Fridshtein, throughout).[5] A ratio of ten to one in half the time. Post hoc...?

Curiously, the American scholar-critic's reaction was less obvious. Scholarship in general depends on other scholarship. And the authoritative stuff that the academics would turn to was—properly so—slow in coming. Agnes Boulton's *Part of a Long Story* came out in 1958, Croswell Bowen's *Curse of the Misbegotten* in 1959. But these were family matters. Memories. Research took longer. Doris Falk's study was published in 1958. The Cargill, Fagin, and Fisher volume came in 1961, bringing together four decades of criticism for potential scholars. That same year Jackson R. Bryer primed the bibliographical pump with "Forty Years of O'Neill Criticism," in *Modern Drama* 4 (1961), 196–216. And the next year Jordan Miller opened the tap completely with his *Eugene O'Neill and the American Critic*. Sophus Winther's and R. D. Skinner's 1930s studies were rushed into early 1960s reprints. But most influential in spurring scholarly activity were the Gelbs' *O'Neill* (1962) and Sheaffer's *O'Neill: Son and Playwright* (1968—the first volume of his two-volume work). These biographies were explicitly the results of the appearance of *Long Day's Journey* (see Note 6). We count 15 books devoted to O'Neill in the decade of the 1960s, among them—besides those just mentioned—work by Doris Alexander, Timo Tiusanen, Egil Törnqvist, John Henry Raleigh, John Gassner, and Clifford Leech. Of the making of books ... saith the preacher. And the preacher could certainly be speaking of books about O'Neill. And what of essays in learned journals? Each of the five years before *Iceman* averaged seven and a fraction essays. In 1957 there were 20. The decade of the 1960s produced an annual average of 16 plus. The 1980s doubled that.

The inference here is not a logical fallacy. The indications are too strong that the *Iceman* and *Long Day's Journey* of 1956–1957 produced results not theretofore thought likely and brought O'Neill's reputation, apparently moribund, but actually only dormant, back to life. And though many great and talented actors attempted O'Neill after 1957, it is clear that Robards' playing of Hickey started it all.

Of course we can't pin everything on performances and productions. Once Jason Robards was established as a stage actor, films were open to him. And however cynical he was about his work in films—he claimed to do them so that he could afford to do stage plays—they are to the public, probably less austere in its tastes, an important part of his career. In effect, for him his stage career was punctuated by his screen career. But to the general public, it was the other way around. We all know that the best-attended stage plays are those with film stars. Robards played Hickey for fewer than six months in a theater that could only have held a few hundred patrons at a performance. At best his stage performances could not have reached more than 50,000 people. The one TV showing of *Iceman* in 1960 could have reached millions. He made sixty-one motion pictures including the 1962 *Long Day's Journey Into Night*; thirty-six television films, including the *Iceman* just mentioned and *A Moon for the Misbegotten* in 1975. And 16 "Notable TV guest appearances."[7] All in a career that began in 1948. After all, Robards' professional recognition—prizes, awards—came because of films. He won two Oscars for best supporting actor two years running (*All the President's Men* [1976] and *Julia* [1977]), an Oscar nomination, again for best supporting actor (for *Melvin and Howard* in 1980). And five Emmys for television productions, only one of which was based on an O'Neill play (*A Moon for the Misbegotten* in 1976). The nearest "the quintessential interpreter of O'Neill's desperate truth-tellers" (Gussow) came to receiving recognition for his O'Neill interpretations on stage were Tony nominations for his roles in *Long Day's Journey Into Night* (1957), *Hughie* (1965), *A Moon for the Misbegotten* (1974), and *A Touch of the Poet* (1978). However the only Tony he actually won was for his performance in the non–O'Neill *The Disenchanted* (1959).

From *Iceman* to *Long Day's Journey* to all the 500-plus other and later O'Neill productions, to the Gelbs and Sheaffer, and to the thousands (literally) of writings about O'Neill and matters O'Neillian, we are much in Robards' debt.

Okay, we know we've played fast and loose with the numbers, but we don't think Jason Robards would mind.

NOTES

1. Quintero did not direct Robards' *Hughie* of 1981 but he had already directed Robards as Erie Smith in the 1964 American premiere of that play. In the case of the 1988 joint production of *Ah, Wilderness!* and *Long Day's Journey Into Night*—where Robards played both Nat Miller and James Tyrone—we assume that whatever influence Arvin Brown's directing of *Ah, Wilderness!* may have had (Brown agreed to be a last minute substitute to take some of the burden from the shoulders of the ailing Quintero) was mitigated by Quintero's. With rehearsals for the one play in the morning, and for the other in the afternoon (McDonough 273), it would be very hard to keep separate not just two characters in two quite different plays, but also two directorial influences.

2. In the United States that is. In Sweden O'Neill seems never to have lacked an enthusiastic audience. The success in Stockholm of *A Moon for the Misbegotten*, just months before his death in November 1953, incited O'Neill to give the Royal Dramatic Theatre first performance rights of all of his so-far unpublished plays, free of royalty payments. The world premiere of *Long Day's Journey Into Night* was in Stockholm in February 1956—three months before its Broadway (and American) premiere (see Williamson). Ironically, during New York's four-year vacation from O'Neill productions, London attempted three—in 1954 *Moon for the Misbegotten*, and in 1955 both *Desire Under the Elms* and *Mourning Becomes Electra* (this last directed by no less than Peter Hall) (*Who's Who* 12th ed., 114, 146, 155).

3. Smith and Eaton's bibliography includes coverage of the English and foreign-language productions from 1973 on, their numbers, the where and when of them, etc. See Works Cited.

4. The eight were *"Anna Christie"* (1925), *The Hairy Ape* (1925), *The Emperor Jones* (1926), *Desire Under the Elms* (1927), *Gold* (1928), *Ile* (1929), *All God's Chillun Got Wings* (1930), *Bound East for Cardiff* (1933). The five were *The Rope* (1958), *Where the Cross Is Made* (1958), *Ile* (1961, a new translation), *In the Zone* (1961), *A Touch of the Poet* (1966). Curiously, the English theatre during the twenty years after 1956 mounted only six O'Neill plays in eight productions—*Iceman, Journey, Misbegotten* (*Who's Who*, 13th ed., 62, 78, 112), *Electra, Hughie* (*Who's Who*, 14th ed., 108, 158), another *Electra* (*Who's Who*, 15th ed., 114), *Mansions* and another *Journey* (*Who's Who*, 16th ed., 27, 101)

5. The number of publications and the amount of foreign scholarly activity in the fifties and sixties are most difficult to document—no organizations like our present MLA had at the time developed the machinery for gathering the necessary data. However I. G. Fridshtein and V. A. Skorodenkoed had attempted an omnium gatherum of Europe-wide scope. Though surely not definitive (and no sane bibliographer would ever claim definitiveness), we think that, if we cannot depend on the accuracy of its absolute numbers, we can depend on the proportions those numbers indicate.

6. Part One of the Gelbs' *O'Neill* is entitled "Haunting Ghosts"; and note the subtitles of both Sheaffer volumes: *Son and Playwright* and *Son and Artist.*

7. The quoted words and most of the data in this paragraph come from the Jason Robards filmography on the internet: <http:// us.imdb.com/Name?Robards, +Jason> Also see <http:// washingtonpost.com/wp-srv/style/longterm/filmgrph/ jason_robards.htm>

WORKS CITED

Atkinson, Brooks. "O'Neill Tragedy Revived." *New York Times* 9 May 1956: 38.1
_____. *"Anna Christie." New York Times* 10 Jan. 1952: 33.1.
Fridshtein, Iurii Germanovich, and Vladimir Andreevich Skorodenkoed, eds. and comps. *Iudzhin O'Nil: biobibliograficheskii ukazatel'.* Pisateli Zarubezhnykh Stran. Moscow: Kniga, 1982.
Gelb, Arthur, and Barbara Gelb. *O'Neill.* New York: Harper, 1962.
Gussow, Mel. "Jason Robards, Actor Who Elevated O'Neill, Dies at 78." *New York Times,* 27 Dec. 2000. <http://www.nytimes.com/ 2000/12/27/arts/ 27ROBA.html>
McCarthy, Mary. *"Moon for the Misbegotten*: The Farmer's Daughter." *New York Times* 31 Aug. 1952.
McDonough, Edwin J. *Quintero Directs O'Neill.* Chicago: A Cappella Books, 1991.
Miller, Jordan Y. *Eugene O'Neill and the American Critic: A Bibliographical Checklist.* 2nd ed., rev. Hamden, Conn.: Archon, 1973.
Quintero, José. *If You Don't Dance They Beat You.* Boston: Little, Brown, 1974.
Sheaffer, Louis. *O'Neill: Son and Artist.* Boston: Little, Brown, 1973.
_____. *O'Neill: Son and Playwright.* Boston: Little, Brown, 1968.

Smith, Madeline C., and Richard Eaton. *Eugene O'Neill: An Annotated International Bibliography, 1973 through 1999*. Jefferson, N.C.: McFarland, 2001.

Who's Who in the Theatre. 12th ed. London: Pitman, 1957.

Who's Who in the Theatre. 13th ed. London: Pitman, 1961.

Who's Who in the Theatre. 14th ed. London: Pitman, 1967.

Who's Who in the Theatre. 15th ed. London: Pitman, 1972.

Who's Who in the Theatre. 16th ed. London: Pitman, 1977.

Williamson, George. "*Long Day's Journey Into Night*: Plaudits for O'Neill." *New York Times* 19 Feb. 1956, sec. II: 1.6.

O'Neill's Cry for Players

by Zander Brietzke

Zander Brietzke teaches at Montclair State University, N.J., and is author of *The Aesthetics of Failure: Dynamic Structure in the Plays of Eugene O'Neill* (McFarland, 2001).

I never saw Jason Robards on stage, but I have a vivid recollection of seeing him in the televised version of *A Moon for the Misbegotten* in the early 1970s with Colleen Dewhurst and Ed Flanders.[1] I was a young teenager at the time. I remember no details from the production, but an impression of profound human suffering, love and compassion has stayed with me to this day. That emotional experience helped through the years to shape my view of theatre. It showed me what theatre could be, and reduced virtually everything else to mere piffle. I have never watched this production again, fearing, I suppose, that it would not measure up to what I think that it was. Instead, I use my memory of that experience as the standard to measure other theatre events. I expect theatre to change my life. I want the theatre event to transform my experience of the world and give me fresh insight about how to conduct myself. If not, then what's the point? And now, when I plunk down up to $65 or more for that experience, my expectations reach new heights, and my patience with the mundane and the ho-hum wanes even further.

I realize now that artistic inspiration on a specific occasion did not solely spark the magic of that production of *A Moon for the Misbegotten*. Robards, Dewhurst and Quintero had been working together for a long time. The production was not a marketing vehicle for the stars, either. In fact, the actors and director were trying to rebuild their careers, calling themselves the Resurrection Company. The Broadway engagement and the recording of the play resulted from the success of the production, not the other way around. The production began very quietly as a work among a small group of dedicated actors and a director who built the production from a foundation of mutual trust and respect. This was not a one-time event, but part of a much larger commitment. Robards developed as an O'Neill actor over a thirty-year period, beginning with Hickey in 1956 at the Circle in the Square. Working with director José Quintero, he went on to play Jamie in *Long Day's Journey Into Night* (1956), Erie Smith in *Hughie* (1964), Tyrone Jr. in *A Moon for the Misbegotten* (1973), Melody in *A Touch of the Poet* (1977), and Hickey again in *The Iceman Cometh* (1985) and finally Tyrone Sr. in *Long Day's Journey Into Night* (1988). Theatre history records many productive alliances between great playwrights and acting companies: Shakespeare and the King's Men; Molière and his Palais Royal troupe; Chekhov and the Moscow Art Theatre; Brecht and the Berliner Ensemble. O'Neill never found a group of actors and a director whom he completely trusted during his lifetime. Posthumously, however, his ideal interpreters, Robards and Quintero, found him.

Mel Gussow's lovely obituary of Robards recounts in full the legendary story of how the actor first won the role of Hickey.[2] He was both too young and too thin for the character described by O'Neill in *The Iceman Cometh*. Nevertheless, Robards insisted that he be allowed to read for the part and in his audition he captured the essence of the character. The irony of this story is that Robards, or any relatively unknown actor, would never be able to duplicate that feat in today's market. His career ascended along with the rise of the Off Broadway and subsequent nonprofit theatre movement. The Circle in the Square Theatre launched that movement into prominence with its 1951 production of Tennessee Williams' *Summer and Smoke*, starring Geraldine Page. The success of Off Broadway theatre at that time epitomized the cliché, "two boards and a passion." What was a passion then has become largely an institutional matter today. The founders of the original theatres have departed leaving the shells of organizations in their wake. The recent death of Robards means much more than the passing of an outstanding actor; it signifies the end of an era and a way of doing theatre that has practically vanished today. One way to honor his tremendous achievements would be to create a new theatre dedicated to the works of Eugene O'Neill, in whose plays Robards created legendary performances, which develops the talents of the actor within a sustained body of work.

Such a theatre might occupy two sites, one stationed on either coast. The eastern theatre would be situated near the Eugene O'Neill Theatre Center and Monte Cristo Cottage in Connecticut. The logical locale on the opposite side of the country would be in Danville, California, near Tao House and the O'Neill estate there. These two indigenous theatres would draw strength from their surrounding environments, either the hard and rocky soil in the East or the open vistas and temperate climate in the West, and cultivate a style and repertory suitable to their particular region. The Tao House Foundation in California recently hosted the first ever Eugene O'Neill Festival in Danville.[3] The program featured a condensed 45-minute version of *Ah, Wilderness!*, a discussion panel among actors who had appeared in O'Neill plays, sea chanteys and sailor's work performed by two men in a barn, a Blemie look-alike contest,[4] and presentations by biographers Barbara and Arthur Gelb and Stephen A. Black, as well as director Arvin Brown. In addition to the Eugene O'Neill Foundation, the National Park Service and several local businesses and industries sponsored the event. The whole town of Danville seemed to get involved and there are future hopes and plans to produce a full-length play and make the festival an annual occurrence.

This successful event offers a preview of what a dedicated and permanent O'Neill theatre might become: a venue to explore the implications of American life through the dramatic prism of its best playwright. I suggest that the only means to move O'Neill production forward in this century is to produce him in a repertory situation in which a dedicated group of artists can mull his works and produce them over time within the confines of a stable environment and a reliable cast of players. Repertory theatre challenges actors to develop and present a body of work within a single season. Imagine the excitement of rotating performances of *Long Day's Journey Into Night, Mourning Becomes Electra, All God's Chillun Got Wings, Desire Under the Elms, The Iceman Cometh, The Hairy Ape*, the early sea plays, *"Anna Christie," Ah, Wilderness!*, and *A Touch of the Poet*. How much would an actor learn in a season? How much would an audience experience during a long weekend?

If the Provincetown Players and Theatre Guild represent the first generation of O'Neill producers, Quintero and Robards comprise the next one. Certainly they set the production standard. Robards tried Shakespeare and the classics for a bit, but despite his success in many different roles, he will be remembered historically for his relationship with O'Neill. Many actors attended the memorial service for him on February 26, 2001. George Grizzard, Elizabeth Wilson, Judith Ivey, James Naughton, Matthew Broderick, Anne Jackson and Eli Wallach, Kevin Spacey, and Sam Robards spoke in loving remembrance and appreciation of his artistry and generosity onstage and off.[5] At the end, a film montage tried to summarize his entire career. Among the clips was an interview with Robards conducted for an upcoming documentary on O'Neill.[6] This was the last interview Robards gave and he was evidently not well and very frail. However, his eyes twinkled when he began to speak of his relationship to O'Neill and he became excited as he talked about the rigors of performing *A Moon for the Misbegotten*, a very long play, eight times a week. He recalled how he confided to Colleen Dewhurst that he feared he could not meet all the emotional demands of the production at every performance. He planned to hold back on some occasions. Dewhurst admitted to him that she felt the same way. And yet, Robards shared the experience of feeling during his performance, when he felt particularly emotionally spent, a hand at his back pushing him forward in the play and encouraging him to perform at his best. Robards referred to this experience as the hand of O'Neill guiding him through the performance. Robards felt the intimacy of this guiding hand only because he had come to know the play and the playwright so well through years of study. That hand is open now and beckons new actors to fill an empty space.

NOTES

1. The play was produced for television and broadcast by ABC Theatre on ABC-TV on Tuesday, May 27, 1975.

2. *New York Times*, 27 Dec., 2000.

3. The festival was held September 22–24, 2000.

4. Blemie, Silverdene Emblem, was the name of O'Neill's prized dalmatian, about whom O'Neill wrote an amusing and touching eulogy.

5. "Fellow Actors Honor Jason Robards," *New York Times* (February 27, 2001), section B, p. 8.

6. The documentary is being filmed by Ric Burns.

PART TWO
Memories and Tributes

George Beecroft Remembers
The Iceman Cometh, *1956*

George Beecroft retired to Costa Rica after 25 years as a writer and editor at the Asbury Park (N.J.) *Press*. His recollections of the O'Neills may be found in Jane Scovell's *Oona: Living in the Shadows: A Biography of Oona O'Neill Chaplin* (Warner Books, 1999).

In 1956, Jason Robards' New York was only an hour away by train from my hometown at the Jersey shore. But the two were worlds apart. New York was the world source of life, liberty and the pursuit of happiness. My hometown, Point Pleasant, by name, was the source of domestic tranquility.

It was in New York that Eugene O'Neill, the godhead of Robards' acting career, got drunk and waxed eloquent at the Hell Hole bar. It was in Point Pleasant that his wife, Agnes Boulton, tried to make a peaceful home for him. In New York, daughter Oona became the toast of café society at Sherman Billingsley's Stork Club. In Point Pleasant, she studied Latin in Miss Ethel Osmond's class. New York is where Shane O'Neill ended his life in a fall from a police precinct window. Point Pleasant is where he raised his family.

In 1956, Robards' world and my world came closer together the night he took the stage in *The Iceman Cometh* and I took the train to New York.

It started at the Old House, the Boulton family homestead, several weeks before *Iceman* opened. I was a fourteen-year-old boy who Miss Boulton depended on to do yard work and run errands. As the son of the town police chief, I had developed a reputation as a young worker who could be trusted. Many of the locals looked at the Boulton and O'Neill clans as "a bunch of Bohemians" but as my father dispelled local gossip with a policeman's penchant for facts, I got to appreciate both families and developed a keen interest in O'Neill's plays.

I loved to work at the Boulton house because Miss Boulton would allow me to borrow books from the family library. While Robards was about to begin his role as Hickey, I had already patterned my life after Richard Miller in O'Neill's *Ah, Wilderness!* Like Richard, I developed a superior attitude from reading a few great authors. And, because of this, I had become alienated from my friends and family.

The alienation was strongest with my father, so I had mixed emotions when Miss Boulton announced that she wanted my father and me to take her place at the *Iceman* opening. I do not know whether it was puberty or my emulation of Richard or both. But to my young mind, my father was the last person on earth that I wanted to share my upcoming theater experience. He never spoke in literary terms about O'Neill and I never saw him read anything other than police reports or hunting magazines. But I reasoned that I could pretend that the man sitting next to me at the Circle in the Square was a stranger and the audience would think the same. We took the train to the city and neither one of us spoke. My father could be just as stubborn as me.

We arrived at the theater in Greenwich Village just as the doors opened and were shown to our seats on the apron of the round stage. We sat in two bar chairs at a small bistro table. The stage was still dark but I could make out the bar and other tables at Harry Hope's saloon.

The audience was an odd mix of suits, ties, and casual clothes. The Richard Miller in me had taken great care in dressing for the occasion: neatly pressed shirt with comedy and tragedy cufflinks and a crisp three-pointed handkerchief tucked in the breast pocket of my suit jacket. I must admit though, it was not really a handkerchief but three small pieces of cloth stapled to a cardboard that said, "One Hour Martinizing." Just as no one knew the guy next to me was Pop, they would be equally in the dark about my faux handkerchief.

I settled into my seat as the play began and tried to look older than my years as O'Neill's genius was given life on stage. Robards reminded me at first of our local pastor. But as he got more into the part, it occurred to me that he was selling these people reality. The Richard in me offered congratulations at such an astute observation. Then, before I could savor my self-praise, everything went wrong.

Robards, sitting opposite me, was in the middle of a long and powerful speech. He took a big drink of water not only to quench his thirst but to provide some silence for his message to sink in. As he resumed, even more powerful than before, his words literally sprayed across the table, covering my face with water.

I was embarrassed and there was nothing I could do about it. Robards continued to spray and I turned crimson, fearing everyone was staring at me. I started to reach for my handkerchief but remembered it was as false as my Richard Miller persona.

I don't know how long the humiliation lasted. It seemed like hours. Then I felt a large hand pass a neatly folded hanky into my hand. Pop to the rescue.

I opened it full and blotted my dripping face. Robards must have realized what had happened and broke character for a few seconds to flash me a grin and a wink.

It wasn't necessary. But I held the handkerchief in my lap for the rest of the play. As we left the theater, my father and I broke our self-imposed silence.

On the homebound train, Pop and I shared our impressions of the play. It was then that I learned that my father was also a visitor to Miss Boulton's library and had read *The Iceman Cometh* the night before the performance. I found that he did a lot of reading during the lonely night shift and from that day forward, thanks to Jason Robards Jr., my father and I were on the best of speaking terms. The topic that was left unspoken was the handkerchief incident.

Travis Bogard, "Presentation of the First Eugene O'Neill Foundation–Tao House Award"

Travis Bogard was Chairman of the Department of Dramatic Art at the University of California–Berkeley for many years and in the 1970s was a leader in efforts to save O'Neill's Tao House from being destroyed. He was host of the meeting at which the Eugene O'Neill Society was founded and was Artistic Adviser of the Eugene O'Neill Foundation–Tao House. His books include *Contour in Time: The Plays of Eugene O'Neill* (Oxford University Press, 1972), *The Unknown O'Neill* (Yale University Press, 1988), and *Selected Letters of Eugene O'Neill* (Yale University Press, 1988), which he edited with Jackson R. Bryer. He died April 5, 1997. He presented the Tao House Award to Jason Robards on November 12, 1989.

Tonight, the Eugene O'Neill Foundation–Tao House presents the first of its planned annual awards to be given to a person who has contributed in a significant way to the American theater.

Some of you may wonder why the award is not more specifically focused and given as an honor to one who has performed or directed the work of Eugene O'Neill with distinction. The Foundation's Board of Directors, however, have preferred a broader basis: the recipient's contribution to the theater in this country. Tonight, of course, we have the best of both possibilities: an actor whose career in the theater has

Jason Robards and Travis Bogard, 1975. Photo by Jere Hageman. Used by the kind permission of the Eugene O'Neill Foundation–Tao House.

been luminous and one whose performances in the Tao House plays have been definitive.

The Board has elected to make the presentation of its award on behalf of the American theater in O'Neill's name. To so use his name is not to take an unjustifiable liberty because it can be held that O'Neill truly created that theater. Before he began his work at the end of the first decade of this century, our theater, which had been founded on British repertory and British acting traditions, was a theater of actors, playing farces, melodramas, and occasional "problem plays" in the somewhat overwrought style that O'Neill's father exhibited as the Count of Monte Cristo.

O'Neill mocked such actors affectionately and used some of their qualities in creating Con Melody and James Tyrone, but there can be little doubt that when his work began to dominate the stage a new energy emerged in our theater. Our stage was significantly altered and was never to be the same again.

Perhaps what O'Neill released in our theater can best be defined as a seriousness of purpose which was felt and responded to by playwrights, and with them, actors, directors, designers, producers and critics. Of course there remained meretricious, silly, and inconsequential offerings, but as the century matured the theater in the United States rapidly began to prove itself as an art. O'Neill was in the van of the new movement. I am not saying that other writers merely imitated O'Neill. Far from it. The years between 1920 and 1950 were much more creative than that; it was a great period in the history of world theater. But each play by O'Neill was a challenge which others had to accept to the best of their abilities.

The essence of that challenge was the constant assertion demonstrated in O'Neill's work that the drama was more than a passing diversion. Through theater, serious matters could be asserted and proved, and actors, directors, designers and all the other artisans of theater were joined in a common enterprise: making the theater matter.

Perhaps this was caused by no more than O'Neill's egocentric belief in himself. To put it politely, he was always self-concerned. But as his plays grew in complexity of theme and technique, he opened doors. Tennessee Williams' Blanche Du Bois is a daughter of O'Neill's Nina Leeds. *The Iceman Cometh* tells the story of the death of a salesman, generating some of the attitudes toward society revealed in Miller's later tragedy. I am not saying that either Williams or Miller owe O'Neill a specific debt, but in the largest sense, they owe him everything. He made the earth on which they were to walk, a good soil for what they would plant there.

As for the actors? Like any great dramatist, O'Neill gave them opportunities limited only by their own lack of imagination and nerve. Like Hamlet, the major roles in O'Neill plays are eagerly sought by good actors. They are a test of an actor's artistry. You will remember Colleen Dewhurst's perception of the danger that waits for an actor taking on an O'Neill role when she said that O'Neill must be acted as if the performer were in the eye of a hurricane. To create an O'Neill character onstage must surely be entirely fulfilling.

It can also be maintained that O'Neill like other great writers for the theater—Shakespeare, Wagner, Chekhov—created the kind of actor he needed. The best evidence for this is the man who sits beside me on this platform, and the service Jason Robards has done for both

O'Neill and the American theater is the reason for honoring him tonight.

Judging from his preserved comments, O'Neill did not think much of actors. He said often that only two actors, Charles Gilpin who first played the Emperor Jones, and Louis Wolheim who created the Hairy Ape, equaled his own imaginative conception of the roles they undertook. At the end of his life, the actors did poorly by him so that neither *The Iceman Cometh* nor *A Moon for the Misbegotten* was fully appreciated. After their closings there was nothing. O'Neill died, and the theater did not expect to hear his voice again.

But there was still strength in the hurricane, and in 1956 at the Circle in the Square, José Quintero and Theodore Mann slated *The Iceman Cometh* for revival. The actor who appeared then as Hickey was of course Jason Robards, and thereafter he was clearly seen as one of the great American stage actors. It was an important moment when Jason and Gene met.

Before *The Iceman Cometh*, Jason's reputation was growing but was not yet fully established. He had appeared in two Broadway plays, *Stalag 17* and *The Chase*. I hope that he will tell you tonight of the circumstances surrounding his being cast as Hickey. It brought him unstinting acknowledgment as a major actor. After that success, the list of others stretches long and includes *Long Day's Journey Into Night* (Jamie), *Macbeth*, Lillian Hellman's *Toys in the Attic*, *A Thousand Clowns*, Arthur Miller's *After the Fall, You Can't Take It With You*, and always, as if they were challenging gauntlets to be picked up, the major O'Neill plays: *Hughie, A Moon for the Misbegotten, A Touch of the Poet*, and most recently, the celebrated revival of *The Iceman Cometh* and a back-to-back production of *Ah, Wilderness!* and *Long Day's Journey* in centennial revivals wherein he played both fathers.

His career on film and television has been equally distinguished and daring. On television you will remember vividly his appearance in *The Day After* as a victim of an atomic explosion and his strong portrayal in *Inherit the Wind* as well as his appearances in several of the major O'Neill plays. On film—well, go to the movies. He's getting impressive reviews for his performance in *Parenthood* at the moment.

Looking at Jason's full career to date, it is undeniable that he has given a dignity to the American acting tradition that is hard to find these days. It can be truly said that in his work as an actor there moves

Top: Jason Robards and Kaye Radovan Albertoni meet at the 1989 Tao House Award ceremony. Kaye Albertoni was O'Neill's nurse in 1936–1937 and thereafter helped both O'Neills during their many illnesses before they left the Bay Area in 1945. Used by the kind permission of the Eugene O'Neill Foundation–Tao House. *Bottom:* Jason Robards and Jane Caldwell Washburn meet at the 1989 Tao House Award ceremony. Jane Caldwell typed O'Neill's letters and manuscripts from 1944 to 1946. Used by the kind permission of the Eugene O'Neill Foundation–Tao House.

a spirit, an energy similar to that which marked O'Neill's career as a writer. The ability to work without ceasing, the refusal to commit to unworthy projects, the continuing creativity, the seriousness of purpose, the certainty, the discipline and the power to move his audience to tears and laughter, sometimes on the same out-breath. In Jason's person as well as his performance, something of O'Neill still breathes. There's no question but that O'Neill would have ranked him with Gilpin and Wolheim as an actor who has realized the playwright's conceptions perfectly.

His success has been attested by many public acknowledgments. In the awards business, he's an old hand. He received a Tony Award in 1959 for best actor and the ANTA Award for an outstanding contribution to living theater. He won an Obie and two Academy Awards as well as the Film Critics' Circle Award for the best supporting actor. In 1976, he received a Presidential Citation.

Testimony to the affection and admiration felt my many national figures for Mr. Robards is not far to seek. Here are a few examples:

From Glenda Jackson, who recently starred in O'Neill's *Strange Interlude.*

From Katharine Hepburn who gave a distinguished interpretation of Mary Tyrone in the film of *Long Day's Journey Into Night.*

From George White, president of the Eugene O'Neill Theatre Center in Waterford, Connecticut.

From the New York producer Joe Papp.

From Jack Lemmon, who not long ago took a flier himself in *Long Day's Journey Into Night.*

From the O'Neill biographers, and *New York Times* writers, Arthur and Barbara Gelb.

From Senator Alan Cranston, a long-time supporter of Tao House.

From Congressman Ron Dellums.

From Congressman George Miller.

From State Senator Daniel E. Boatwright.

From President George Bush.

Jason, the award we have for you tonight is nothing you need. Your mantle shelf groans with awards. What it is is a bronze medal of the gate of Tao House which when opened reveals an engraving of O'Neill's face. I'm sure you'll forgive us, Lois, for giving you one more thing to dust. We hope that you will both recognize that this model indicates that the real gate to Tao House will always be open to the two of you. Jason, you will understand that we at Tao House are deeply indebted to you and that we must give you this as a token of our admiration, respect and affection for what you have done for us all, both as workers at Tao House and as a small segment of your world-wide fan club.

Arvin Brown Remembers

Arvin Brown, former Artistic Director of the Long Wharf Theatre in New Haven, directed Jason Robards as Nat Miller in the
1988 *Ah, Wilderness!* at the Yale Repertory Theatre.

All actors have unique ways of rehearsing. Some go through the
agonies of the damned, feeling a day's work done if they have sobbed
through lunch break and wept much of the remaining afternoon. Not
Jason Robards. America's greatest tragic actor had within him a mysterious imp, whose duty it was to break up his colleagues whenever
possible. Colleen Dewhurst lived in terror of the giggles that would
consume her if Jason looked at her the wrong way, and he looked at
her the wrong way on a daily or even an hourly basis. Jason's imp also
checked out the director just to make sure he was properly responsive
to whatever acting moment had just passed. Jason could so delight
himself with a bit of comic business he would stop rehearsal cold to
share his joy all around, leaving his fellow actors to wonder how such
a major player could slide so easily in and out of a scene.

Woe to the actor, however, who underestimated the power of
Jason's concentration once the rehearsal process was over and the run-
throughs and performances began. Jason would then be stunningly
and absolutely present, and one would recognize how hard he had been
working beneath the laughter and the games.

It took me a while to understand the secret behind what could
be a madcap rehearsal process. Actors have always been more successful

than most in preserving the child within. In Jason's being, the inner child was perfectly preserved in all his innocence, seeking approval when he felt he deserved it, yet possessing the knowingness that only great artistry can bring. Therefore Jason's imp could celebrate accomplishment with a simple wonder that seemed to say, "Isn't acting fun?" and "Aren't we lucky to be doing it?"

And so actors who performed with Jason could watch him snicker and snort his way to tragic heights. When they allowed themselves to be enveloped in his spirit, when the sheer magic of acting with Jason had worked its miracles, they too might catch a gulp of the pure air at the top. And at that point why not throw a look or two at the director to see if he had managed the climb along with them.

Zoe Caldwell Remembers

Zoe Caldwell played Mary Tyrone in *Long Day's Journey Into Night* opposite Jason Robards in 1976 at the Brooklyn Academy of Music. She won Tony Awards for her performances in *Slapstick Tragedy* (1966), *The Prime of Miss Jean Brodie* (1968), *Medea* (1982), and *Master Class* (1996).

Jason Robards and Zoe Caldwell read from *Long Day's Journey Into Night* at Connecticut College, April 2000, during the *Eugene O'Neill's New London: Influence of Tme and Space* project. Used by the kind permission of the photographer, A. Vincent Scarano.

131

Dearest Jason,

I thank God I am not an actor who has the range to play Hickey in *The Iceman Cometh*, Jamie in *Long Day's Journey Into Night*, Erie Smith in *Hughie*, and James in *A Moon for the Misbegotten* because I would be defeated before I even began.

My love, my loss,

Zoe

Douglas Campbell Remembers

The Scottish-born actor played the king in Tyrone Guthrie's celebrated *Oedipus Rex* of 1955. A regular at the Stratford Festival, he recently directed Wycherley's *The Country Wife*, *Julius Caesar*, and *The Alchemist* at Stratford, played Falstaff in Vancouver in 2000, and in the 2001 Stratford production of the Henry plays.

It was so extraordinary listening to the gravel-voiced American clashing his way through the Shakespeare text of Hotspur. However, the true honesty of the interpretation and his personality made this characterization one of the best I remember in this role.

His warmth and clear sensibility made him one of the most attractive human beings it has been my pleasure to work with. And I remember Jason Robards with respect and deep affection. A splendid actor and friend, I hope his contribution to the drama will not be forgotten. For certain, I will never forget him.

Wendy Cooper, "Jason Robards, Jr., and Eugene O'Neill's Tao House"

> Wendy Cooper is President of the Eugene O'Neill Foundation–
> Tao House in Danville, California, and a maker of documen-
> tary films.

"I visited Tao House and a tremendous serenity came over me; it threw me, and carried me through," Jason Robards Jr. commented when visiting Eugene O'Neill's California home in November 1989. He was there to receive the Eugene O'Neill Foundation's Tao House Award. He added, "This award and the visit to Tao House almost made me cry ... and I never do cry. I have a hard time crying even when I'm acting."

"I was very moved when I saw the door open and saw Mr. O'Neill's face [in the bronze Tao House Award]. I can only tell you he gave me life. I didn't know where I was going. I lived through some strange times, until I met Eugene O'Neill. I could not live; then I started living. All wild and crazy things are documented on stage with O'Neill."

Jason Robards was the first recipient of the Tao House Award, presented by the Foundation to those who have served the cause of the American Theatre with distinction. In presenting the award, the late Travis Bogard, the Foundation's artistic director, recognized Jason Robards as "an actor whose career in the theatre has been luminous and one whose performances in the Tao House plays have been definitive.... He played in *The Iceman Cometh* in its New York revival and then in *Long Day's Journey Into Night* as Jamie—hence bringing about an O'Neill revival and starting a really great career for himself as an O'Neill artist."

Travis added, "Jason has a spirit and energy and ability to work, as well as artistic certainty, discipline and the power to move (the audience)—the ability to work without ceasing with creative artistry, tears and laughter. In Jason's person and performance something of O'Neill lingers. There's no question that O'Neill would have ranked him with Charles Gilpin in *The Emperor Jones* [one of the two actors O'Neill admired] as an actor who realized the playwright's concept."

Jason had been a strong supporter of the Foundation since the early seventies, mounting a benefit performance of *Hughie* to raise money to purchase Tao House. Asked in 1989 why he decided to do the benefit, Jason said, "Because Darlene Blair and Lois Sizoo wrote a letter. My wife Lois picked it up and said, 'Jason this is really important, this is something you should do—you should do *Hughie*.'"

Founding members Darlene Blair and the late Lois Sizoo remembered the event in a 1996 interview: "What prompted the benefit was the need for $200,000 to buy the house. Jason was a friend of Travis. We wrote a letter, didn't hear, didn't hear, and then the agent called and said, 'where the hell have you been?' (Darlene was on vacation) Then it was action here and a lot of work. Jason and Jack Dodson were wonderful men and actors—we had a marvelous time with them."

Bill Blair recalls that when he and Darlene picked up Jason and Lois from the airport to take them to a reception at Dave and Marj Humphreys' Alamo ranch, "It took us 45 minutes to get from the gate to the baggage area. He was so kind and accommodating to people wanting autographs."

Bill added that Dave Humphreys showed Jason his workshop with all the latest equipment. Jason commented on a curved welded rod, "What's this, a divining rod?" When Dave's answer was "yes," Jason said, "you're putting me on." So Dave directed Wes Sizoo, Bill Blair, Jason and Jack Dodson to walk up the hill and draw a line when the rod dipped downwards. Jason said, "Oh, come on," but when it worked he was captivated and had Dave make him a dozen to give away as gifts.

Jason Robards and Jack Dodson, backstage during a 1975 production of *Hughie* performed in San Francisco for the benefit of saving Tao House. Used by the kind permission of the Eugene O'Neill Foundation–Tao House.

Jason had known Travis Bogard since 1964 when he was on his original road trip with *Hughie*, appearing in San Francisco at the Curran Theatre. Travis, in 1993, recalled, "I'd met Jason when he toured with *Hughie*. I'd asked him to come to talk to my class [at UC Berkeley]. It was at 10 A.M., which was hard for him. He said 'I'm a night person,' but he talked very ably and charmingly and then we had lunch. He afterwards offered to bring *Hughie* with Jack Dodson and put it on here. I was Chairman of Dramatic Art at Berkeley and had access to the Zellerbach Auditorium, so in late spring or early summer we put on *Hughie*. Henry May, the resident designer at the Dramatic Art Department, who also did work for Omnibus TV in NY, did the set. It was sold out. Jason and Jack were so pleased they took it to LA to the Westwood Playhouse and all the proceeds went into the Foundation coffers."

The production in Berkeley was organized in three-and-a-half weeks. Lois remembered, "Darlene and I drove all over the Bay area selling two-for-one tickets—it was not a lot of money, about $10,000 profit, but the performance won critical rave reviews, so Jason and Jack took it to Los Angeles."

An article in the *Oakland Tribune* by Robert Taylor said, "For Robards returning to *Hughie* is like meeting a friend for the first time in a number of years, the same person, yet not the same. Not that the character he plays is a decade older. 'He seems just where you are,' Robards observed, 'where you are in life.'"

Sylvie Drake in "Stage Notes" in the LA *Times*, July 3, 1975, wrote: "There was a benefit Saturday in Zellerbach Auditorium and everybody came. They would have been fools not to. The combination was unbeat-

Jason Robards and Jack Dodson in a doorway on a visit to Tao House, 1975. Used by the kind permission of the Eugene O'Neill Foundation–Tao House.

able: Jason Robards and Jack Dodson 're-creating' the Broadway opening of Eugene O'Neill's *Hughie* with proceeds from the top ticket price of $50 going to the Eugene O'Neill Foundation, Tao House, for the preservation of the playwright's former residence in Danville, California, as a theater center. It was an affirmation—if one were needed—that Robards is a definitive O'Neill interpreter, an actor of infinite sensibility who understands the playwright's people by instinct rather than intellect.

"Rumpled hat on his head, red necktie like a noose around his sagging collar, Robards plays none of the obvious (but all of the right) manifestations of Erie Smith.... Emotionally, Robards maps out the concealed man, foregoing outer gesture for the much truer inner one: a spare but present alcoholic cough, the pleasureless consumption of a 'meal' on the lobby floor, the use of that elevator cage to intimate other cages of quite another sort...." The columnist also noted, "At the reception Mrs. Robards talked about their children, four-year-old Shannon, their girl, and ten-month-old Jake O'Neill Robards, whose middle name is for daddy's favorite playwright."

In a 1989 news conference, Jason remembered the 16 performances in Los Angeles, September 28 to October 12, 1975, and the $100 a seat gala opening attended by stars like Walter Matthau and Lauren Bacall, and talked about his partnership with the late Jack Dodson—"We were partners for 22 years, longer than any of my marriages" (at that time).

Lois Sizoo said, "Jason's career at that time was at a standstill. He had been not drinking for a year. He was living in Beverly Hills and hated it. He called it Beverly Depths. He'd finally found the right wife, Lois O'Connor, but hadn't had any major roles for some time. After this performance, good things happened. It was an historic performance. He won the role in *All the President's Men*, which earned an Oscar, and his career seemed to change. He calls Mr. O'Neill 'the old man.' He has a great affinity for Mr. O'Neill."

Foundation members enjoyed a cocktail party in 1975 after a rehearsal of *Hughie* at the St Francis Yacht Club. Director Emeritus Al Gentile had this remembrance of Jason Robards and *Hughie*:

"To me Robards is important on a personal level: that he treated me and my students with an unforgettable grace and scholarly manner, without seeming bored, on one summer afternoon. I would like to add the name of Jack Dodson to that afternoon's events. But let's get to that day on the Cal campus.

"My summer school classes had just gotten underway, when one evening in midweek, I got a call from Lois Sizoo. She asked a favor of me. Was it possible for me to bring my students to a dress rehearsal of O'Neill's *Hughie*? The two actors in the play, Robards and Dodson, wanted the feel of a live audience and its reaction. ... about 30 of my students saw a fantastic performance by two outstanding troupers in a most interesting two-character play.

"But what the youngsters enjoyed even more than the play was going backstage and spending more than an hour talking to two wonderful and learned gentlemen...." In a column following Jason's death, Al remembered sitting on the steps of Tao House prior to the performance with Jason, staring at the barn across the way.

He says, "There is one thought about our conversation that stayed with me: I asked about his performance preference—whether he liked being in Hollywood or onstage in New York. He answered 'Hollywood is the place where I work. The theater is where I live, and that's what I find in O'Neill—the place where I live.'

"The memory of meeting with Jason Robards is a memorable and pleasant one. What a rare encounter—sitting on the stairs of a famed playwright's home talking with a Hollywood star. Indeed, this was truly a rare occasion," Al added.

Following their successful run of *Hughie* benefiting Tao House, Robards and Dodson united to perform the play again at the Academy Festival Theatre in Chicago in August 1976.

The proceeds from the performances of *Hughie* enabled the Foundation to put a down payment on Tao House. But Jason's role with saving the house and having it designated a National Historic Site did not end there. In 1976, he went to Washington with Lois and Darlene to give a statement at a Senate hearing.

In their 1996 interview, Darlene and Lois recalled, "We had written letters to all the senators on the committee and called on them in Washington to tell them Jason was coming to testify. He was in Hollywood doing retakes for *All The President's Men*. He flew all night on the red eye and wouldn't let us pay [Wes Sizoo and Bill Blair paid for their wives' airfare]. All the senators' aides had said that 'those people' all say they are coming and never do. It was great to walk into that hearing with Jason and see their faces, and he was so eloquent in his testimony. He said there are so many battlefields that are National

Historic Sites, how about having some for playwrights? The Senate voted yes by voice vote."

In October 1976 the bill designating Tao House as a National Historic Site was signed by Gerald Ford after passage through both houses. The state initially owned the house but transferred it to the Park Service in June 1980.

Jason continued to support Tao House, by giving a benefit performance of *The Iceman Cometh* in the Lunt-Fontanne Theatre in New York in 1985. Proceeds went to the National Park Service for the Tao House furnishings plan. At the time Lois Sizoo was quoted as saying, "He is an old, old friend of the Foundation.... He is probably responsible more than anybody else for saving the house."

The following are Jason's words as he accepted the 1989 Tao House award: "Dear friends of Eugene O'Neill, thanks for inviting me, and for the splendid opportunity to view the progress of the Foundation and the Park Service at Tao House. Special thanks to Craig Dorman, superintendent of the Eugene O'Neill National Historic Site, for the tour. I share this honor with all of you. It represents the progress you have made, most particularly, and reflects the courageous dedication and indomitable crusade of Darlene Blair and Lois Sizoo. If you had witnessed the pint-sized dynamo Darlene filibustering Strom Thurmond and the Senate, you would know the truth. Thanks Darlene and Lois. Another inspiration was Travis. We met in 1964 when I was doing *Hughie* on the Broadway road show. I admire him, and use *Contour in Time* as a reference all the time. Travis Bogard and Jack Dodson, Mary Dodson and my wife Lois (Lois and Mary worked to put the Los Angeles set and production together) worked on and off to make Tao House possible.

"I share this award with members of the Foundation. The vision and dedication of members of the Foundation is not merely saving our literary heritage; but like Eugene O'Neill, through dramatic works, you will inspire future generations to an understanding and appreciation of all humanity."

In an interview he further elaborated on why he believed in the importance of Tao House. He could see the benefit historically: "When I went there I found serenity of some kind; there's somebody there. I feel other people may feel the same—It's almost mystical." He believed in the importance of Tao House for O'Neill's plays: "It's important for

Jason Robards and Jack Dodson in O'Neill's study at Tao House, 1988. Used by the kind permission of the Eugene O'Neill Foundation–Tao House.

all his works—the fact that we have Tao House there for writers, actors, performers. And we don't always have to do O'Neill. It can develop like other festivals. Playwrights' Conferences should be there.

"It's great for people who love theatre. It's important to continue with these things. Being an actor is 98 percent rejection, but the fact is that many people are interested in communicating and performing, and here they have to have a place to do it," he added.

Speaking about acting O'Neill, Jason said, "O'Neill has a habit of bringing things out of you you didn't know were there. "I had an unhappy childhood; my father was an actor who did marvelously well and sort of sold out his craft. I had a younger brother, I went to sea, I became a boozer (for me it was in my mid-thirties after I had some success). We both had drinking problems. Now I go to Tao House and it is the same period as my house. 'Why are these things coming at me?' There are the same things in the kitchen as we have; we both have views, though ours is of the ocean, not the hills. I have a different feeling now than the first time I was here. Now it's back to the way it was in O'Neill's time, it's different."

Speaking about acting O'Neill, Jason said, "I erased all his stage directions when I was doing *The Iceman*, fortunately with pencil. I got in so much trouble I started erasing the erasing. O'Neill is so specific with his attitudes and characters. The directions are part of the play. He'd been an actor; he knew the actor and it's evident. It's like driving down a highway; he lays out every turn."

Director Emeritus Carol Lea Jones remembers meeting Jason at the Award dinner: "What can you say about Jason Robards that the whole world hasn't already said in praising this wonderful and gifted actor? I think of him as O'Neill's best friend. He was a best friend to Tao House…. In 1989, the Foundation awarded the first Tao House Award to Jason…. He graciously agreed to come to Danville to receive his award. After the invitations were in the mail, the big earthquake hit the Bay area. The event had to be postponed a few weeks, but Jason adjusted his busy schedule saying to Lois Sizoo, 'You know, Lois, the show must go on!'

"He enjoyed the tributes heaped upon him at this event…. Letters of congratulations were presented to him from our prestigious Honorary Board members, from his many friends and fellow actors, … and politicos who helped Tao House to get Historic Site status…. I was fortunate to read a short and funny letter from Glenda Jackson (including the words, 'you're the best') and did he ever laugh heartily at her wit! That is how I will remember him as a fine and generous man who enjoyed life, laughter and anything O'Neill. My one regret is that at the end of the evening Jason asked me to join him and his wife and others in the bar for a drink. Unfortunately my table of guests were in a hurry to leave so I regretfully said no. I should have made my guests wait in the car!" Carol added. Among letters read at the ceremony congratulating Jason on his career was one from the eminent producer, the late Joseph Papp:

Dear Jason

If Gene were in the audience tonight, I know the old grump would crack a smile. He might even admit that he was pleased, that you, a mere actor, was being honored in his name.

Knowing his opinion of actors, this admission, however, would not have come without some grinding of teeth.

Yes, the old Irishman might even have had a tear in his eye, saying that he loved you, my good man, as we all do.

Chin up, shoulders straight, you deserve the honor.

George C. White of the Eugene O'Neill Theatre Center stated, "You have been a major force in bringing O'Neill's plays out of the mist of obscurity and making them immortal parts of our theatrical heritage." The late Senator Alan Cranston recalled working with Jason when he pushed for Senate passage of his bill; and laudatory letters were received from many, including President George Bush, Katharine Hepburn, Congressman George Miller, O'Neill biographers Arthur and Barbara Gelb, and actor Jack Lemmon.

In September 1986, Jason Robards had visited Tao House for a day-long conference organized by Travis Bogard of west coast directors sharing ideas for the centennial year. During the centennial year, 1988, Jason played in back-to-back productions of *Ah, Wilderness!* and *Long Days Journey Into Night* at the Yale Repertory Theatre and was excited about the number of young people who were involved.

He was last at Tao House in April 1991, on a free day from shooting a TV mini series, *An Inconvenient Woman,* at Filoli, Woodside.

Jason came to introduce fellow actor Peter Gallagher to Tao House. Peter had played Edmund Tyrone with Jack Lemmon in the Broadway production of *Long Day's Journey Into Night.*

The visit illustrated how Tao House was important to Jason Robards—and Jason Robards was important to Tao House. He was a mainstay of support for the Eugene O'Neill Foundation and the National Park Service as members worked to establish a living memorial to the great playwright. His legacy will remain—but his brilliance, his friendship and warmth and his support will be sorely missed.

Blythe Danner Remembers

Blythe Danner won the Theatre World Award for her work in Molière's *The Miser* and was nominated for a Tony for her performance in *A Streetcar Named Desire*. She co-starred with Jason Robards in a 1996 production of Harold Pinter's *Moonlight* at the Roundabout Theatre.

I was nervous on the first day of rehearsal for *Moonlight* at the Roundabout. I was to play Jason Robards' wife in that production and wondered how I'd be received, perceived by that great actor—I think our greatest. I had been so moved by his brilliant performance in *A Moon for the Misbegotten* with Colleen Dewhurst that I couldn't get up from my seat afterwards, so overcome with emotion was I. It was absolutely gut-wrenching, so real. His pain was so palpable. I think in those days his life and his art wove themselves into a most complex dance of depth.

But every performance Jason ever gave at any point in his life I know was imbued with a reality and commitment that were unparalleled. I thought he must be a very complex man. So to be introduced to this open-faced, sunny, almost boyish person who instantly and wholeheartedly welcomed you into his "club" was an extraordinary surprise. He started a conversation as if he were picking up and continuing one he had begun the other day with you, sharing personal stories, leaning in for some intimate detail meant only for you—or so it seemed—just happy to have a co-worker to share with and to swap a good tale with, though there was little swapping at first—I sitting there in awe, just basking in his presence.

He was the quintessential American—easy, fun—without a drop of pretense. He was inclusive with everyone, the least vain actor I've ever worked with. He was as interested in protecting your performance as his own; actually, yours seemed to be more important to him. One could say that seemed shrewd, but I honestly believe that Jason was without any artifice. He was sincere.

I think of him nearly every night when I'm on stage, any stage, and I feel his presence inspiring me. I often marvel that such a great artist could be without moodiness, demanding temperament, or difficulty. He was completely at ease with himself and he put his fellow players at ease. He is sorely missed. They don't make 'em like that anymore.

Richard Allan Davison, "Memories of Jason Robards, Jr., Actor's Actor"

Richard Allan Davison, Professor of English at the University of Delaware, co-edited *The Actor's Art: Conversations with American Stage Performers* (Rutgers University Press, 2001).

I first talked with Jason Robards after a Saturday matinee performance in *Park Your Car in Harvard Yard*. He greeted me at the stage door and walked with me to his dressing room at the Music Box Theatre in New York. We talked about his acting career, especially his Tony Award-winning involvement in the 1958 production of *The Disenchanted*, a play based largely on Scott and Zelda Fitzgerald. Relaxed and old-shoe comfortable, he talked about the importance of Andrew Turnbull's biography of F. Scott Fitzgerald in his portrayal of Manley Halliday, how moved he was especially by the last line regarding Zelda's death by fire eight years after Fitzgerald's own sudden death: "In those flames she died her second death and was buried in Rockville beside Scott, where she belonged." Robards and Rosemary Harris (as Jere) captured exactly the destructive power of Scott and Zelda's mutual love. His Manley Halliday brought alive both Fitzgerald's early bright promise and the sense that at his death "the sword had worn out the sheath." I remember the fierce struggle in Robards' voice and body as the phantom of a youthful Jere appeared shortly before Halliday's death: "Jere, that dress—it's on fire! It flashes and shimmers" and then "'Take her away! Take her away! This woman is smothering me."

The cover itself of the 1958 *Playbill* of *The Disenchanted* captures the nuances of their performances. Rosemary Harris stands behind Robards' seated figure, her right hand draped casually yet possessively over his dark-jacketed left shoulder, her fingers slightly splayed. Her left hand holds aloft a feathery boa-like fan. Her eyes are closed, her head tilted back, her lips parted in a haughtily triumphant smile. The expensive string of pearls winds once around her neck and drapes down below the clinging waist of her silver, form-fitting flapper dress. Jason's eyes stare straight ahead out of a face that is slightly haggard and deeply haunted. His jaw is set, his shoulders slumped forward, and even the waves of his hair seem like a fist clenched.

In his performance, he struggled with the destructive threat of her intoxicating insouciance. I recall Robards' gleefully guilty drunken smiles, his fearful bursts of temper, how convincingly he aged twenty years and then became a romantic twenty-three again in alternating scenes of past and present, moving from bright promise of youth to frustrated sense of failure, of loss, culminating in the wisdom of his scribbled death-note to his protégé, warning him against wasted youth: "A second chance—that was our delusion. A first chance ... that's all we have. Remember that, laddie—."

On this day, however, Robards' first words to me were in praise of his fellow actor in *Park Your Car*, Judith Ivey: "Isn't she wonderful? This is her play!" Such tributes were characteristic of Robards, and he always sprinkled our conversations with theatre anecdotes and tributes to the work of other actors. When I recounted my memory of Christopher Plummer (as the Bastard in *King John* at the Stratford Shakespeare Festival in Canada) snatching a script from an audience member sitting in the front row, he laughed heartily and said, "We did that all the time at Stratford—after each performance we'd say, 'How many did you get tonight?'" Then he recalled the best performances: "Alfred Lunt, Freddy March (in *Gideon*), Thomas Mitchell, Olivier (in *The Entertainer*), Nicol Williamson (in *Inadmissible Evidence*)— 'Did you see him?! Actors should be a little mad'—, Christopher Plummer (in *Arturo Ui*)." Of Pinter's *Moonlight* he said, "Blythe

Danner is going to play the wife, and I love her." He talked of the rewards of acting with Colleen Dewhurst, how she had greeted him forty-five years before in the green room of the American Academy with her dazzling smile: "That smile will live forever despite her death on August 22." Jason Robards Sr. not only remained one of his favorite actors of the past but also an inspiration in the present: "I love my dad. He was the one constant in my life. He was my best friend." He loved working with good actors and they loved working with him. Maureen Stapleton mentioned Robards and George C. Scott as actors she felt safest with: "You're not as good as when you're playing with them." George Grizzard is unequivocal: "Of all the actors who influenced me [the most] Jason Robards did.... Jason Robards is the most exciting actor I've ever been on stage with."

My own view is that the rugged grace in Robards' performances perfectly blended his distinctive husky voice and sinewy fireplug body. He made the baritone timbres of his indelibly haunting voice and the controlled lurch of his body perfect instruments for such different characters as Hickey, Jamie, Con Melody or Murray Burns or Ben Bradlee, or Manley Halliday, or Dashiell Hammett or Howard Hughes or Odysseus or a dying old man in *Magnolia*. Our conversations made it evident that he was at home not only with O'Neill but with Scott Fitzgerald, Hemingway, Homer and Shakespeare (he "thoroughly enjoyed" playing Hotspur in Stratford, Ontario, and looked forward to the challenge of Lear, albeit with a slender, light Cordelia). What a Lear he would have made!

I have other memories of such brilliant performances as Murray Burns in *A Thousand Clowns* where he charges the opening scene with pure gnomic charm as he turns in profile and looks slyly skyward. Jason's wonderful rendition of "Yes Sir, That's My Baby" echoes in the mind as does his ride with Barbara Harris on their bicycle built for two to the tune he sang with his own banjo accompaniment on the soundtrack. (A hard act to follow, the scene prefigured Paul Newman's and Katharine Ross's tandem bicycle ride pedaled to the tune of "Rain Drops Keep Falling" in *Butch Cassidy and the Sundance Kid* several years later.) With small touches, he illuminates Murray's quirkily charming humanity, such as in his jaunty bongo drumming on the table to reinforce a moment of independence, or the flip twirl of his attaché case as a gesture of rebellion. He makes his reluctant lockstep joining of the early morning marching office workers less a surrender to conformity than his acceptance of the overriding importance of his nephew's well-being.

Another brilliantly sustained performance was in the love-hate scene with his younger brother in *Long Day's Journey Into Night*. Robards' energy and stumbling control, his physical and verbal violence, his love-filled resentment over the success his brother may achieve that will elude him forever, embraced a bravura performance in the best sense. In complicitous delight he twisted on the light bulb that their frugal father had just twisted off, momentarily undoing the paternal darkness. He waggled the top of the whiskey bottle under his brother's nose in rhythm with "I love your guts, kid." He tapped his finger on the top of his glass in deliberate cadence to "The Old John Barley Corn." Then with his thumb hooked on one suspender strap he danced in place a few stuttery steps of a jig. He picked up his brother and sat him down firmly in a chair on "Listen to me," then picked him up again and shook him on "I can't help hating your guts," and then embraced and hugged him and declared his love, then added "Be on your guard," and "I hate myself," then walked across the room, sat in a chair in profile, looked back at him and intoned, "God bless you kid." Robards moved through this scene of many emotions, sustaining both power and believability in a transcendent performance.

Jason Robards had a gruff but gentle, no-nonsense way of making me feel welcome during each of the visits we had, mostly in his dressing room. Once when a stagehand brought him lunch I excused myself and got up to go, but he waved me back to keep him company. He made me feel a welcome companion to one who was very welcome company. When in mid-sentence he dropped a plump hamburger on his dressing room floor, he calmly bent over and picked it up, eyed it, brushed it off and put it back between the top and bottom of the roll, took a big bite and chewed with pleasure as he contemplated my question about Christopher Plummer between the matinee and evening performance of *No Man's Land*. I last talked with him at Princeton at a reception after his beautiful reading from Robert Fagles' translation of *The Odyssey*.

Back to our first visit: shortly before, he had sent me a very moving letter (dated December 18, 1991) about my piece in *Playbill* on Ian

Charleson's brilliant performance of *Hamlet* for the National Theatre in 1989, a role Charleson took and played knowing he was dying, a last performance less than two months before his death. Jason wrote that he was "incredibly moved" by the account:

"How I wish I had been there with you and Annie to see his perfect *Hamlet*! For some reason, I did not know of Ian's death or his taking on the role of Hamlet—especially in the terminal stages of his illness. Maybe it is because the ravages of the AIDS epidemic have robbed us of so many great talents in all the artistic creative fields that I hide my head in the sand sometimes so as not to be heartbroken again.... it seems to me that Ian's courage and passion will outlast all of us."

Certainly the best of Jason's film work will outlast all of us. Would that the same were true of his magnificent stage performances which survive only in the memories of those who saw and heard them. For me and those who were there, they include many of the most priceless milestones of the last forty-five years of American theatre history.

Thank you, Jason Robards.

Robert Einenkel, "A Movie Struck Young Man Discovers Theater"

| Robert Einenkel teaches drama at Nassau Community College.

I had made it! I would be going to the School of Performing Arts as an acting major, a boy from Queens whose entire sense of acting and theater was derived from local movie matinees, radio melodramas, singing in the choir and other church shows, and a one-time role in a Long Island amateur theater production as an adorable 11-year-old. I had never actually gone to the theater, only movies.

What advice or instinct guided my mother and father to decide that it was time that I actually saw real actors in real productions I do not know. But one evening I found myself, accompanied by my mother, in a balcony seat of a Broadway theater about to see *Long Day's Journey Into Night*. Neither of us knew anything more about the play than that it was supposed to be "good" and, with the exception of the movie star Fredric March, the actors were all unknown to me.

For four hours, I watched a family of actors walk, talk and drink on stage and not much more than that. In movies anything that length would feature chariots or parting seas or masses of men battling each other for the honor of God or Rome. I doubt if I intellectually understood more than half of what I was watching—I was around 12 years old—but I was mesmerized nonetheless. That mere conversation amongst people who represented the ordinary family categories of father, mother and sons could prove more exciting and dramatic than any physical spectacle I had witnessed in the movies quite astonished me.

And then came that special moment in Act IV. Jamie, the older brother, returned from his drunken debauch, so besotted his ability to stand seems possible only through an angry act of self-will, confesses to his younger brother and warns him against himself. I had already fixed on this actor and his character because of his enormous charm and his entrancing voice that rang crystal clear even to our balcony seats. His warmth and humor made him so seductive a presence every time he was on stage that he seemed to be the one Tyrone removed from the worst pain the family could inflict.

Here he was, however, violently threatening, darkly tortured by inner guilt at his desire to destroy his own brother. The transition was astonishing, as if the actor had ripped off an outer skin to reveal a skeleton-like ghost underneath. And, then, almost as quickly as this ugly figure had appeared, the actor character had restored his charming veneer.

Never had I seen anything so impressive, this ability to transform oneself almost instantaneously and to inhabit a character with such conflicting traits. Rarely have I seen it since.

This Jason Robards performance was my introduction to great acting and was the beginning of my own transformation from a casual desire to act to a serious need to participate in theater at its most revelatory level.

Footnote: In 2000 I finally had the temerity to direct a production of the play with a student cast where I teach, Nassau Community College. Many were skeptical of the possible results of such a production. I was certainly crossing my fingers. In the end, however, as it must have been for Robards, O'Neill's masterpiece seemed to pull everyone involved up to their best level of work and leave actors and audiences deeply affected by having lived with these tortured souls for a few hours.

Sheila Hickey Garvey, "For Jason 'Jamie' Robards"

I had an old theatre program from the 1920s with Jason Robards' father's name in it and I'd been telling Jason that I was going to give it to him. Somehow, I hadn't gotten around to it. He kept asking me to call him and I had been busy. Then, a year ago last November when I heard about Jason's cancer, I decided to check up on him. I got Lois on the phone and expected to express my concern to her only and hang up. But when Jason found out it was me, he got on the phone and insisted that I come on over to his home the following Tuesday. He said he was just "sitting around thinking too much" and he "wanted company."

When I got there, I found that Lois had been on duty taking care of him day and night and hadn't allowed herself to leave him even to do a bit of shopping—which she loves to do. I became her excuse to get out for the afternoon and Jason got a chance to tell his stories— which he loved to do—and I became his rapt audience. Mostly he told tales that he had told before—but somehow, maybe it was just because he had been so recently sick, or maybe because he was at home in the comfort of his living room—there was a sense of intimacy about his way of being with me that had an immediacy to it. He knew his time left on earth was limited and he wanted to get the stories he told as right as he could get them. It was such an intense afternoon that, at one point, when a wind storm that was happening outside blew open one of the windows in the room where we were sitting, he started. We'd just been talking about Carlotta O'Neill. I said it was her entering the room. Jason got quiet and his body shuddered.

We talked about everything from his current medical state which he said, with conviction, was "this time, not my fault." He described Lois' unwavering attention to him during his hospitalization and afterwards, which he repeated with awe. He couldn't believe he deserved to be treated with such devotion. She even got him to go to church sometimes. Lois O'Connor he'd say; he loved the fact that she was Irish.

He had a bad history with women. He segued into alimony jokes, which reminded him that he needed to earn more money so he could leave it to his children. He kept reiterating that he had to be responsible. This was because earlier in his life there had been those times when he hadn't been. He said he missed being able to hang out in New York. He said it wasn't as much fun to go into the city anymore. People didn't hang out at the Lambs Club or the Players anymore. This reminded him that he used to check into the Chelsea Hotel after performances while he was doing *Hughie*. He said he was compelled to do that. He couldn't stop himself. Then he did some of Erie Smith's monologues for me. He became visibly afraid and began to shake. He said, "If Erie didn't stand there and talk to the night clerk, the poor devil would probably go up into his room and jump out the window."

Jason kept calling me "Dr. Gaaahhvey." He'd try to sound like Tallulah Bankhead—"Gaaahhvey" and he'd put the sound in his throat. Then he would play on that even more and talk to me about his depression. After all, to Jason, a doctor was a doctor was a doctor. He was a scamp even when sick and discouraged. He loved a good joke.

He asked, "How's the Society doing?" meaning the Eugene O'Neill Society. He played with the word Society—Sooo—sigh—hotty. Sensitive to the nuances of words, he was intimating that putting O'Neill and Society together was more than a bit absurd.

He took time, a lot of time, to look through the program I brought him—respectful time—and he noticed details about the way theater programs were printed in those days that provided me with a tour of the history of theater at the dawn of the last century. He knew his theater—then and now—not just O'Neill. He knew the classics. He wanted to do *Lear*. He told me about the years he took off to work in Canada with the Stratford Shakespeare Festival. He'd gotten bad reviews which said he would never be a classical actor and so he went to Canada to improve his skills. He said the people from the Stratford

At the O'Neill Society meeting, the Modern Language Association Convention in New York, 1991. From left, Stephen A. Black, Jason Robards, Sheila Hickey Garvey, and Geraldine Fitzgerald. Used by the kind permission of the photographer, Gary Vena.

Festival were still his friends. They even took care of his children when his wife, at that time, was ill.

Seeing the program I brought him caused him to muse about his feelings towards his father. At one of our O'Neill conventions, Jason was reminded that he was once angry at his father. This had upset Jason. Jason kept telling me how much he loved his father and how proud he was that he had been able to bring him back to Broadway to act with him in *The Disenchanted*. Jason began to look back on his youth. Jason had left home after high school just to get away from his family's pain. He ended up joining the Navy and then World War II broke out. He was trapped again. Jason talked about being at Pearl Harbor on December 7th. When I sympathized with that, he said he thought he had actually "lucked out." He had been in boot camp with men who'd ended up in the Philippines in the Baatan Death March. Jason preferred Pearl Harbor.

He talked about the fact that when he first acted in the O'Neill plays he had absolutely no idea how much they paralleled his own life—and youth—and childhood. He had no idea. He'd gone to acting school and had learned all that "art is a mirror of life stuff" but he wanted me to know that he really didn't know. It wasn't until he was sober and in *A Moon for the Misbegotten* that he began fully to realize how close his own life had been to the roles he played. The realization still filled him with awe.

We talked for hours. I told him we were swapping stories—he liked that. When Lois came back, she looked relieved that he was still alive. He was such a visceral man. He saw that look in her eyes. He felt guilty that she had to be so tied to him—but he was glad she was and he kept telling her so. Just like the characters he played, he was afraid to be alone.

Lois and Jason took me on a tour of their O'Neill collection. It fills two corridors of their home. It's unique and fabulous. A movie poster of his father (he was indeed handsome enough to be a matinee idol); a David Hays rendering for the set for *Hughie*; a photo someone took of Colleen Dewhurst holding him in *A Moon for the Misbegotten*. The photo showed Josie taking on Jamie's pain. It's a photo that equals a Michelangelo in what it captures of Colleen's soul. It's a magnificent photo. Jason bowed his head after he looked at it. He turned away from it—it hurt too much. Lastly, Jason showed me a copy of the text of *Long Day's Journey Into Night*. It was one that Carlotta gave him, one she personally inscribed. It read to "Jason Jamie Tyrone from Carlotta Monterey O'Neill." Even then, Carlotta knew.

Jason's afraid we'll forget him. He saw what happened to his father—his career had stalled, his wife left. He was forever despondent. Today we call it depression. Jason was so afraid that the same thing would happen to him that he never stopped working—even though he could. He was driven by his past. He loved his father. His father's pain taught Jason how to love. Jason became the father figure he wanted to have himself—he protected all of us, by exposing his pain and analyzing it, by fostering O'Neill's work, by protecting José Quintero's fragile identity, by treating his friend Colleen with respect. Jason ran towards his feelings.

As my visit began to wind down, Jason walked me to the door of his home; the oxygen tube connected to his nose trailed behind him. I kissed him goodbye. I checked with Lois first. She said it was OK. He opened the door and a burst of wind suddenly swept leaves around his feet. He thrilled at the sudden force of nature and voraciously sucked some air into his lungs. He said with full intent, "Ah—fresh air." He stood relishing his breathing as I drove off. When I looked back at him, he was framed in the doorway of his home. He saw me and our eyes locked. Jason loved living—he appreciated every breath.

George Grizzard Remembers

George Grizzard received the Tony Award for *A Delicate Balance* (1996). He spoke at the memorial service for Jason, February 26, 2001.

I started studying acting with Jason 43 years ago. Beginning in 1958, we did three plays together on Broadway, a couple of TV shows and a not-so-hot movie. And I learned something each time. Jason was, for me, simply the best actor I've ever been on a stage with. The most alive, the most generous, the most honest and the most fun. Acting with him was a refresher course in excitement ... in the way we thought it was always supposed to be. I don't know anyone who ever worked with him—or even knew him—who didn't love him.

Our first play together was an adaptation of Budd Schulberg's great novel *The Disenchanted*. There was a terrific scene in the second act of the play between the two writers we were playing. We were asked to do it on "The Ed Sullivan Show." We shared the program with Johnny Ray, Senor Wences and a dog act. We did our scene, came off to thunderous applause (of course) and stood in the wings. We were exhilarated and exhausted. There were chairs there—eight of them—but the dogs had beat us to them. Eight chairs, eight dogs. I think we went next door and had a drink.

Jason got a Tony for *The Disenchanted*. I got a nomination. The next play I did with him I also got a nomination. Then for 35 years I didn't get a nibble. Again, he taught me something: Don't try acting without him.

In 1961 we did Hugh Wheeler's first play, *Big Fish, Little Fish*, with Hume Cronyn, Martin Gabel and Liz Wilson in a wonderful cast directed by John Gielgud. I don't know whether you remember this or not, but Jason used to drink. And he was pretty good at that, too. One evening I came to the theater just at half-hour, having rehearsed a TV show all day. The stage manager said to me euphemistically, "Jason's a little under the weather this evening." And I said, breezily: "Don't worry. We've worked together before. As soon as the curtain goes up, he'll be fine." Well, I hadn't seen him. He'd had a costume fitting in his dressing room all afternoon for an upcoming movie, *Tender Is the Night*, and had decided to mix bourbon with the boredom of it all. He was deliciously bombed and out to have a real good time. I remember as he made an exit, he turned to Hume and said, "You're gonna kill me when this is over, aren't you." The next day the contrition was biblical: navy blue suit, necktie, hangdog look and the most heartfelt apologies.

In those days, the Tonys were broadcast only locally, from the ballroom of the Waldorf. I lost again, and after the ceremonies my date and I were having a consolation drink in Peacock Alley, the Waldorf's lounge. "Last call" had been made when I looked up and there was Jason, who had probably watched the Tonys at some Broadway watering hole. He was tieless, wearing a rather tired trenchcoat and fedora, feeling no pain ... and carrying a shopping bag in one hand. He joined us, ordered a drink and was told that "last call" had been made. "I've got a *@!%!*" he smilingly snarled at the waiter, pulling one out of his trenchcoat pocket. The drink was brought.

"I've got something for you," he said. "What?" "Your Tony." And here's what he produced: a fifteen-inch-tall, copper-colored replica of the Statue of Liberty, complete with a clock in the base and a functioning flame lightbulb in the torch. I've cherished it for 40 years.

In 1972, the Kennedy Center produced *The Country Girl*, with Jason and Maureen Stapleton. John Houseman directed, and again I got to be onstage with this man. We moved on to Broadway and Los Angeles. There was still one "bad boy" matinee. We in the cast referred to it as "Black Wednesday." But it wasn't too bad. By the time Jason's third-act drunk scene came, he was sober.

After *The Country Girl* came a terrible car wreck and a dance of death. But he survived, with a lot of help and love from Lois and his family and friends. He quit the booze and started a new life. He said to me later, when we were doing that not-so-hot movie: "It was a great day for me when I finally realized that I didn't HAVE to drink." It was a great day for all of us when he quit.

If you were to list his achievements, SURVIVAL would have to be way up near the top. But think of his others: Jason 3rd, Sarah, David, Sam, Shannon, Jake. An Obie, an Emmy, a Tony, back-to-back Oscars, the National Medal of Arts, the Players Club Lifetime Achievement Award and the Kennedy Center Honors.

They are the prizes. But his real achievement was the love and respect he engendered in audiences and in those of us who were fortunate enough to know and work with him. We will not see his like again.

A. R. Gurney Remembers

> A. R. Gurney attended the Yale School of Drama and is the author of many plays, including *The Cocktail Hour* (1988), *Love Letters* (1989), and *Ancestral Voices* (1999).

I knew Jason Robards mostly in the context of my play *Love Letters*. He performed it many times and in many places, usually with Elaine Stritch or Colleen Dewhurst. He seemed to enjoy doing it, and heaven knows, he did it well. I believe he and Elaine were the first older actors to be cast in this play, and together they opened the door for a wide range of ages. Jason got a particular kick out of the Navy scenes, and liked to exchange sea stories with me after his performances. He was a wonderfully engaging guy as well as a first-rate actor. These qualities displayed themselves in the ease with which he performed his part and the natural way in which he navigated through some of the traps of the role. We used to talk a lot about O'Neill, too. He told me the way he absorbed O'Neill's characters and mastered their lines was to read the plays over and over again. He made me think more about my own work and to attempt to write things which might have to hold up under this kind of careful scrutiny and absorption. Naturally I tried to get him to do other plays of mine besides *Love Letters*. There was talk of *The Cocktail Hour* for a while, but I think the main character was a little too genteel for Jason's tastes. I kept pointing him to the blue-collar underpinnings of the role, but Jason didn't buy any of that and was probably right. When he was recovering from his

Jason Robards at a directors' conference, Tao House, 1986. Used by the kind permission of the Eugene O'Neill Foundation–Tao House.

recent illness, we sent him *Ancestral Voices*, which I was sure he'd like and hoped would be easy for him to do, but I should have known the part of the grandfather was too small and restricted for the likes of him. Like many other distinguished American actors, Jason, to the best of my knowledge, never performed in England. "At least do *Love Letters* there," I said to him one time. "Naw" he said. "If I go to England, I want to go standing up."

Shirley Knight Remembers

Shirley Knight won the Tony Award for *Kennedy's Children* (1975) and also appeared in *Landscape of the Body* (1979), *Losing Time* (1979), and *The Young Man from Atlanta* (1997).

I did *The Country Girl* with Jason on the NBC Hallmark Hall of Fame. It was a wonderful experience and I only wish we had had many more like it. He was always such a gentle man and so generous in the work. We clicked immediately and felt like the married people we were playing. He was a "real" actor but not necessarily a "Method" actor. We did the work. We played. We listened and responded. The result was remarkable. We spoke often of doing a play together but never did. I am sorry now as I know it would have been terrific. I saw the last play he did on Broadway and went back afterwards to see him. It was as if no time had passed since our last meeting, which was twenty years before. I will miss him.

Daniel Larner Remembers

A director of the Eugene O'Neill Society, Daniel Larner teaches drama at Fairhaven College, Western Washington University, in Bellingham. He has recently written a series of articles on the relationship between theater and the law.

I never saw Jason Robards in an O'Neill play, but I remember a muggy, mid-summer day in 1958, give or take a year, that I walked west on the south bank of the Charles River past the Harvard athletic fields to a pavilion, canvas-covered, as I recall, the site of a summer theatre whose name has dissolved for me in the soup of my under-graduate memories. There were two productions, both Shakespeare (in America, new playwrights hibernate in the summertime), and the director was José Quintero.

One was *Twelfth Night,* an astonishing production which began with a single, sustained musical tone of radiant purity wafting through the air of an empty stage. It was no clarinette, no flute, no oboe. This gorgeous, almost unearthly tone was emanating from Russell Ober-lin, the short, plumpish, impish, redhaired, crewcut counter-tenor, who skipped onto the stage with Feste, the Clown, and who was advertised in the program as one of the "fool's zanies." The other "zany," equally additive to the original script, was the magnificent, six-foot-five-inch, blackskinned, bassvoiced dancer, Geoffrey Holder. The rest of the pro-duction tried valiantly to live up to this beginning.

The other production featured Jason Robards as Macbeth. And

what a Macbeth he was. In Act I, Scene 4, speaking of the late Thane of Cawdor (the one Macbeth "enseamed … from the nave to th' chops"), Duncan the King says this: "There's no art/ to find the mind's construction in the face/ He was a gentleman on whom I built/ An absolute trust." And the next words in the text are: "Enter Macbeth." When Robards entered, I saw a Macbeth of size and grandeur, one who you might believe "with bloody execution … carved out his passage" through the enemy. And here was a man large enough to earn Duncan's new trust, and to embrace the boiling evil which too quickly overtakes him.

Above all, here was a man who somehow, in all his military glory, did not know himself. Robards played a Macbeth sucking in his environment, inhaling it and letting it out warmed, surrounded by his moisture, as if he lived only on the life around him. If Macbeth cannot minister to his own disease, it is only because it is so deeply in him, and Robards took it in with every breath, every scent on the sticky Charlesbank breeze, and exhaled it altered, infected, bewitched.

Quintero had his players using the raked aisles (on one of which I sat, near the back) as exits and entrances, and whenever Robards came by, laboring uphill from the stage, he wheezed loudly in the wilting summer heat, sprayed sweat from his armored costume, and heaved for air. I thought he might collapse. But in this intimate, almost off-stage glimpse of the actor, asthmatic or out of shape, I understood the character. Macbeth's breath was more than labored, fetching, desperate; it was the "mouth honor," the widening hollowness, which his own sense of loyalty and nature condemns ("which the poor heart would fain deny, and dare not"), but which he can only keep trying to fill, sucking in life with every step.

In the shell made of Robards' courage stood Macbeth himself, whose corruption of a nation becomes a tale told by an idiot, and whose life becomes a walking shadow. It was Robards' genius to show us this abyss, this colossal emptiness, not just at the end, in those wonderful soliloquies, but somehow in that magical, first-act moment: "Enter Macbeth."

Paul Libin, "Jason Owned the House"

> Paul Libin was the Producing Director of the Circle in the Square Theatre from 1963 to 1990. Since 1990 he has been the Producing Director at Jujamcyn Theaters.

I moved from Chicago to New York in 1951 with ambitious plans to become a professional actor. My very first night in New York I ventured to Greenwich Village to see an actor from Chicago, Sydney Stevens, who was appearing in a production of Federico García Lorca's *Yerma* at the Circle in the Square Theatre in Sheridan Square.

In 1951 the Circle's work was unknown. It was the first theatre I experienced without a proscenium arch. The stage was in the center surrounded by theater seats. That production of *Yerma*, directed by José Quintero, included the soon-to-be-acclaimed Geraldine Page.

I never imagined then that my destiny would bring me to work with José Quintero, Ted Mann, Jason Robards, Geraldine Page, George C. Scott, Colleen Dewhurst, and so many other extraordinary talented artists who became legendary alumni of the Circle in the Square. I abandoned my plans to be an actor in 1955 and worked as a stage manager. In 1957 I produced my first play.

I well remember in 1956 when Eugene O'Neill's *The Iceman Cometh* opened at the Circle in the Square. Brooks Atkinson's review had acclaimed Jason Robards and credited Jason for revealing nuances in Hickey which James Barton, the original Hickey, had not found. Atkinson had said, "Jason Robards Jr. plays Hickey, the catalyst in the narrative, like an evangelist. His unction, condescension and piety introduce an element of moral affectation that clarifies the perspective of the drama as a whole. His heartiness, and his aura of good fellowship give the character of Hickey a feeling of evil mischief it did not have before." I remember that Jason's presence on stage was like a thunderbolt. His portrayal of Hickey was mesmerizing. I wanted to watch him forever, hoping the performance would never end! I saw Jason's Hickey three or four times. I recall seeing him later in the winter of 1956 in *Long Day's Journey Into Night*. The production was acclaimed by all critics and theatregoers alike—"Standing Room Only"—the dramatic hit of that season! Luckily I was able to secure a standing room ticket. Every time I saw Jason before that night and every performance after, I always questioned my decision of giving up being an actor. Not that I could have matched Jason's talents, but he certainly was inspirational. His artistic accomplishment was the yardstick to measure perfection—the ambition of every serious actor.

It was always a treat to see Jason in a play. For me it was best when Ted Mann and I became partners in 1963 and we produced Eugene O'Neill's *Hughie* with Jason as Erie Smith directed by José Quintero. It was a personal triumph for Jason, the toast of Broadway, San Francisco and Los Angeles. Now I could watch Jason whenever I wanted to. Each time I saw his Erie Smith, it was spellbinding!

To see Jason on film and television was invariably an affirmation of his extraordinary talent. It was always a thrill to see him anywhere and hear that deep resonant voice greet me with "Hello Pablo!"

In 1988 the Circle in the Square celebrated Eugene O'Neill's 100th Birthday. The stage setting for the production of Tennessee Williams' *The Night of the Iguana* was too much "Mexico" for O'Neill. We needed something to make the setting more appropriate. From the prop closet some book props that had been in storage were brought to the stage. A large bound ledger was opened to add to the setting for Jason's presentation of the "Hickey" monologue from *Iceman*. The "ledger" was a collection of full-size bound copies of the *New York Times* from the 1940s. It was opened prophetically at the very page of Brooks Atkinson's 1946 review of *The Iceman Cometh*. That coincidence was haunting, as if O'Neill's spirit had come to celebrate his 100th Birthday.

Jason's death was a sad loss. At a memorial tribute to Jason at the *New York Times*, deep felt remembrances and remarks by Barbara and Arthur Gelb and John Darnton, the cultural Editor, were shared with a capacity audience. That tribute also included film excerpts from an interview Jason had with Ric Burns, for his documentary on Eugene O'Neill. Jason spoke, in the film, of his own career as an actor, of O'Neill, and of his insights into the O'Neill characters he portrayed. One rarely experiences an actor revealing how they plumb the depths of the characters they portray. The intimacy of that process and the honesty of his own life experience confirmed the extent of his artistic commitment. It enriched every memory I had of all his great performances.

To this day, when an actor or "civilian" snaps their fingers, I can remember that first sighting of Jason as Hickey snapping his fingers—that tremendous portrayal, that historic performance.

There will always be actors who discover the characters of Eugene O'Neill's plays and who think they make the individual characters which O'Neill wrote their own. But for me, Jason owns the house!

Lois McDonald Remembers

Lois McDonald is Associate Curator of Monte Cristo Cottage in New London

I long admired Jason Robards and was deeply moved by his compelling interpretations of Eugene O'Neill's characters. I especially recall Jason's visits to the Monte Cristo Cottage, O'Neill's boyhood home in New London, Connecticut. He was a faithful and true friend of the Cottage from the time it was purchased by the O'Neill Theater Center in 1974 until he graciously accepted the first Monte Cristo Cottage Award in October 2000. It was surely fitting that Jason, the foremost interpreter of O'Neill onstage, should be the first recipient of this honor.

Through the years Jason followed developments at the Cottage and was especially interested in our programming for teachers and students, designed to make O'Neill more accessible and vibrant for young people. He also was pleased with our play readings and discussion series and generously shared his ideas and suggestions.

His visit to the Cottage in the late 1980s was unforgettable. It was then that he came to film scenes from *Long Day's Journey Into Night* for a television documentary. Jason arrived early enough to spend time talking with Sally Pavetti and me about the Cottage and the upcoming O'Neill centennial celebration, in which he was to participate. He was glad that the restoration of the Cottage, which had begun in 1978, was progressing smoothly. It was then that he told of first seeing the Cottage in 1956, at the time of the New York premiere of *Long Day's Journey*. José Quintero had brought the cast to see the Cottage and so they were apparently the first actors since the O'Neills to spend time in Eugene O'Neill's boyhood home.

It came time for Jason's scenes to be filmed, and I always will recall it as my most memorable dramatic performance. It seemed far more than a performance—it was as if we suddenly were transported back to August 1912 and Jason, after donning his paisley dressing gown, became James O'Neill. He seemed discouraged as he walked through his dark back parlor into his small, low-ceilinged living room and began to tell of his bleak childhood, and the pathos of his unfulfilled dreams. There was a change in the Cottage's atmosphere. For those of us present, it was as if the O'Neills were listening, and the tension was so palpable that we felt transfixed. It seemed one of those times when, as O'Neill said, "For a second there is meaning"—and there was, if only for a brief moment.

Whenever I enter the Cottage I see Jason sitting at the table, suffusing the house with James O'Neill's spirit. I suspect that he is now somewhere with Ella, James, Jamie, and Eugene.

Theodore Mann Remembers

Theodore Mann and José Quintero were founders of the Circle in the Square, the theatre most associated with the development of Off Broadway in the early 1950s.

In the beginning years of the Circle in the Square we were performing in our new Off Broadway theatre on Sheridan Square, a former nightclub. Our plays were performed in the round—what was actually a three-sided performance space. We had done *Summer and Smoke* with Geraldine Page and Lee Richardson in 1952, directed by José Quintero to great acclaim. *Summer and Smoke* is recognized today as the production that give birth to Off Broadway.

This was almost fifty years ago—a long time ago but in my remembrances some events are as vivid as if they just happened today—like meeting Jason. We were casting the male lead in a new play by Victor Wolfson, *American Gothic*. We were excited—a new American play telling an American story. The female lead was already cast, Clarice Blackburn, who had appeared in Broadway plays. We read a lot of actors for the lead and then Jason appeared and easily got the part. He was dark-haired, with a square lantern jaw and he looked like a character in a Norman Rockwell painting. He also had a rakish way about him as though he was cut from the same cloth as Clarice but was different, as if he didn't belong.

The rehearsals went smoothly and we had photos taken of all the cast members. They were posed in front of a stone wall to add a sense of grave austerity. The wall was in Isabelle Halleburton's tiny court-yard on 35th and Park. Isabelle was José's assistant. But Jason was elusive about being photographed in a show. We had photographs taken of each individual cast member but no photographs of Jason. Perhaps he thought that if he allowed himself to be photographed a jinx would be brought on him.

Recently I have been going through our archives to assemble material. In *The Iceman Cometh* file there are only two photographs of Jason. One is with Farrell Pelly, the wonderful Harry Hope of our 1956 production. Interestingly, both of those photos were also taken offstage in one of the second floor rooms above the theatre, not on the set. We have many photos of the cast in rehearsal and production but none of Jason onstage. There is a single snapshot of him in front of the theater's poster: Jason is in civilian clothes, with that mug, that grin which is as wide as a street. There he is, as Hickey, the salvation man, Jason with that twinkle in his eye, the salesman who always makes the deal. That smile, that grin, that wink, are all further proof that Jason and Hickey were one.

About a year ago, I was at a benefit at a college in Connecticut. Jason read some O'Neill, a selection from *Long Day's Journey Into Night*, in which he performed James Tyrone; his voice still had so much timber and warmth in it, and vulnerability. In O'Neill roles he had a heart-breaking need to be believed with his arms down or outstretched, cupped palms baring the essence of himself in the character. He had some kind of magnetic pull that made an audience feel they wanted and needed to help him. After the reading, Jason showed me the script he had under his arm. It was the one he used in our production. There were Jason's notes on most of the pages with heavy underlining for his role. In all the recent revivals of O'Neill's plays that I had seen performed I always hear his unmistakable cadence and that wonderful growl. It's a voice that has haunted every successive production and haunts me still. I long to hear it again. At that same benefit performance, Jason showed me something that he had saved all these years. Slipped into one of the pages of the playscript he had brought to the reading was a ticket from the Circle production of *Iceman* showing the ticket price at $1.50. Jason recalled with relish, "and we did all of that with so little money."

At that event and at another event last October which we both

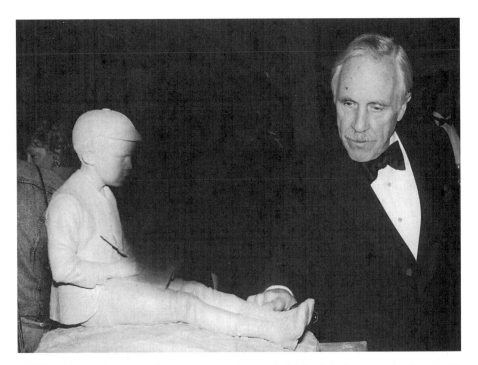

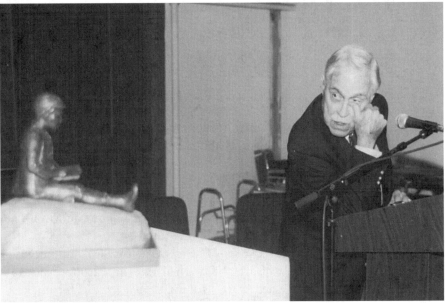

Jason Robards at the Eugene O'Neill Theatre Center, in October 2000, receives the first annual Monte Cristo Cottage Award, a replica of a sculpture of the boy Eugene O'Neill. The boy looks out over the water near the New London train station. Used by the kind permission of the photographer, A. Vincent Scarano.

attended to dedicate a plaque at Eugene O'Neill's birthplace on Broadway and 43rd, Jason and I again exchanged stories from our past. As we spoke that day, I remembered that Jason maintained his name as Jason Robards Jr. even after his father died, as a tribute to him. It wasn't until many years later that he dropped Jr. from his name. During one of our last conversations, I reminded Jason about an incident which occurred during *Long Day's Journey into Night*. We had opened to tremendous success and one day Jason called me to come to his house. He was having trouble at home. He needed someone to watch his children. Of course, I went over. Later, when I got back to the theatre the show had already started. It was during the scene near the climax of the play when Jason, as Jamie, says, "tie a can to me." I remember the way Jason integrated his personal pain and joined it with the emotion of the character. That night's performance was one I can never forget.

When we did *Hughie* in LA, Jason came back to the theatre after a long lunch at the Brown Derby with John Carradine. It was pretty clear that both of them had taken a few drinks. They promptly entered a competition of diction and projection. One jumped up on the stage while the other stood at the back of the empty house. Judging each other's projection, Jason won hands down and Carradine gracefully acknowledged the victory and stumbled back to the Brown Derby.

During *American Gothic*, Jason and I had become friends and we'd talk theatre over coffee or lunch. He told me about being at Pearl Harbor the day of the bombing and about his father whom he spoke of with tenderness and whom he loved dearly and admired not only as a father but as an actor. After *American Gothic*, Jason disappeared for a long time—I think he was on a national tour of *Stalag 17* playing a small part. When he came back he told me how hungry he was for a challenging role, a part that he could bite into.

We had finished casting *Iceman* except, at the last minute, just before rehearsals were to start, the original lead had dropped out to do a film. Amongst the actors we had auditioned to read for Hickey was Jason and he and all the others were rejected. We had an emergency meeting of the Board of Directors in our second floor office to discuss our severe dilemma. I said, "Without the right Hickey we can't do this play!" Someone came into the meeting and told me Jason was downstairs and had to see me. When I came down, he said he wanted to read again and before I could say no, he launched into some of the lines. I could tell he had had a couple of drinks but as I heard him reading the lines I felt a shiver go through me—no one had come close to what Jason was doing. He pleaded to read the part again. I immediately went upstairs and told the group and José what had happened. I said, "There's something special coming from Jason now." José went down to the theatre alone. A half-hour later José came back exhilarated and said to telephone Mr. Robards and "ask for Hickey." We had found our Hickey. We began rehearsals the next day.

Joe Morgenstern,
"Goodbye, Tumbleweed"

Joe Morgenstern is film critic for the *Wall Street Journal* and lives in California. His obituary for Jason Robards is reprinted from the issue of January 6, 2001, with the kind permission of the author and the *Journal.*

A "tumbleweed" is what Jason Robards used to call the character with whom he was most closely identified, the tortured, alcoholic actor Jamie Tyrone in Eugene O'Neill's *Long Day's Journey Into Night.* The desert imagery is just as apt for Robards, who died last week at the age of 78. His acting style was astringently dry, and ineffably fragrant.

Both qualities intersect during a magical passage in the film *Melvin and Howard,* a comic fantasy with Robards as a mangy-haired, half-crazed Howard Hughes. Hughes has wrecked his motorcycle and almost killed himself on the desert. Now he's being driven back to Las Vegas in a pickup truck by Melvin Dummar, the amiable goofball who found him lying in the dark, and took him to be a desert rat. As dawn breaks, Hughes rolls down his window and inhales. "Greasewood," he says with pleasure. Melvin, rolling down his window, inhales and says: "Sage." Hughes grins, with an expansiveness that was one of Robards' hallmarks: "Nothin' like the smell of the desert after the rain."

For an actor who valued theater above film, Robards left some memorable screen performances. He was a definitive desert rat in Sam Peckinpah's beguiling Western *The Ballad of Cable Hogue*. (After four days without water, and in the midst of a sudden sandstorm, Cable rails at God: "You're about to get my dander up!") As *Washington Post* editor Ben Bradlee in *All the President's Men*, he listens to Watergate reporter Bob Woodward complain that "We haven't had any luck yet," then dismisses Woodward, and Carl Bernstein, with two little words: "Get some." Similarly, his Dashiell Hammett in *Julia* snaps, as Lillian Hellman complains of her problems with writing: "Just don't cry about it."

Jason Robards could make few words count for many. Such was the power of his voice, however, that he could make many, many words—as in an eruptive O'Neill monologue—soar and sing. Close your eyes, listen for that inimitable voice, and you can still hear its range, all the way from a baseline of old-fashioned American plain, through rueful or pensive or plaintive, cranky or snarly, puckish or scornful, to tender, rhapsodic or rageful, the sort of magisterial rage that his Jamie Tyrone unleashed against an indifferent world in *Long Day's Journey*. His vocal range reflected the size of his spirit. It was no coincidence that he did so well with O'Neill's vast, rolling speeches, or that a young contemporary artist with a fondness for epic scale, the filmmaker Paul Thomas Anderson, cast him as the central figure in *Magnolia*. Earl Partridge, a TV executive, is dying of cancer, and writhing, on his death bed, with regret over a life ill-spent. ("The goddamned regret," Earl moans. "THE GODDAMNED REGRET!")

That was the last time we saw Jason Robards on the big screen. He'd been battling cancer himself, and it was a shock to see him looking like a death's head, eyes hollow, mouth open, gasping for breath, his spirit seemingly reduced to his still-commanding voice. But what we saw was, in fact, a great actor acting. He'd been terribly ill, but he was improving when he shot the film, and using his recently gained intimacy with the Grim Reaper to enrich his performance.

Some would say that his performances were also enriched by his legendary drinking, that it made him an authentic O'Neill hero. He drank extravagantly, for a very long time, though he managed to stop years ago, banishing booze from his life. But he wasn't Jamie Tyrone, he only played him. His demons were his own, and, for whatever those drinking days may say about him, friends remember him not as an angry drunk but as a funny, playful and sweet one, just as fond of good company when he was in his cups as when he was stone sober.

Playfulness informed his performances; perhaps that's why he could swing, with giddy velocity, from one emotion to its polar opposite. Back and forth, for instance, between Earl Partridge's lacerating regret and his lovely, airy recollections of first meeting Lily, the wife he habitually betrayed, when they were both 12-year-olds in the sixth grade. Pomposity was his target of choice. One friend recalls him lacing zestfully into a fellow actor who, while living in London, equipped his limousine with a gadget supposedly favored by the Queen—a mechanical hand, for waving back at admirers without exertion.

Robards was easy to admire, but not always easy to appreciate, since he had a way of effacing himself. ("I shall give acting back to the performing seals," Jamie Tyrone says lustily.) He had no airs about himself as an artist, though he was a singular one. He liked to learn his lines by writing them out in longhand; all the layers and shading of feeling came later once the words were solidly in place. But the words weren't all; there was always the music, sung or unsung, of a lyrical soul. In the same dawn-time passage of *Melvin and Howard*, Jason Robards does sing, hauntingly, a chorus of "Bye Bye Blackbird." But that's only after Melvin has ordered his passenger to sing and Robards has protested, grumpily: "I have an aversion to song." Untruer words were never spoken.

Sally Thomas Pavetti, "He Never Turned Me Down"

Sally Thomas Pavetti is Curator of Monte Cristo Cottage in New London. "Just Me N'You" is used with the kind permission of the Yale Committee on Literary Property. The poem was previously published in Eugene O'Neill, *Poems*, ed. Donald Gallup (Yale University Library, 1979).

I can't remember when I first met Jason. It seems he was always there, in performance on stage, visiting the Monte Cristo Cottage for filming, or on many other special occasions having to do with Eugene O'Neill. Jason was an event but with no pomp or circumstance attached. He arrived and set about his business, and telling a story or two of his own to any and all who might listen. Everyone was listening.

All of us have enjoyed his oft-told story of his first acquaintanceship with Eugene O'Neill. As a Navy man in World War II (seven years), he found himself crossing the Pacific many times and during one of those long interludes asked if the ship's library had anything interesting to read. He happened upon Eugene O'Neill's *Strange Interlude* and was convinced it was a dirty book, until he read the play and according to him, he was "hooked" on Eugene O'Neill then and there. When Jason tells a story, he always has a glint of mischief in the telling and will look at you quickly to see if you enjoy the story as much as he does. He does and we do.

Over the years, I have seen Jason perform in *Iceman, Hughie, Moon, Touch of the Poet, Ah, Wilderness!,* and *Long Day's Journey Into Night.* Jason Robards ranked as a major interpreter of Eugene O'Neill from the beginning. What was it about the juxtaposition of player with playwright? To me, the master American dramatist performed by the master American actor added up to the essence of American drama. All Eugene O'Neill's plays are distinctly American. They reveal the essential truth of the American spirit, be it the "lie of the pipe dream" or "the hopeless hope." Only in America are there dreams and hope even for the misbegotten.

When Jason talked about doing Eugene O'Neill's roles, he said he was very happy playing Theodore Hickman (Hickey), Cornelius Melody, or James Tyrone Jr. (Jamie). When discussing James Tyrone Sr., Jason said he had done the role three times but never felt "comfortable" or felt that he "had it right." However, on the occasion of the conferring of honorary degrees by Connecticut College to O'Neill biographers Barbara and Arthur Gelb (April 2000), Jason and Zoe Caldwell did a scene from *Long Day's Journey* as part of the ceremony. The audience was spellbound. No one stirred. Of course, thunderous applause. So there, Jason. So there! You had it as "right" as could be.

It has been my pleasure over the years to be asked to invite Jason to speak at the Modern Language Association meeting in New York, as well as to participate in the 1995 Eugene O'Neill Conference organized by Fred Wilkins in Boston. Whenever I asked Jason, he never turned me down. Lois Robards was pivotal in securing Jason's assent. On these occasions there was no mention of a fee or any other demand. At the New York meeting, the lure for Jason was lunch at an Italian restaurant prior to his appearance at the Hilton. (Lois Robards said Jason loved Italian food.) On that fateful day there was a snowstorm. Fred Wilkins and I were aghast, and waiting at the restaurant in misery. However, on cue, Jason arrived, having driven himself from Connecticut. Lunch ensued, many cups of black coffee were poured, and Jason strode on stage at the Hilton to a standing ovation.

The Boston Conference had no culinary lure. However, it had eminent biographers Barbara and Arthur Gelb and the beloved José Quintero. Jason accepted.

The last time I spoke to Jason was at the Monte Cristo Cottage's O'Neill October Festival where Jason was to receive the Monte Cristo

Award for lifetime achievement in the theater. He had been to hell and back with operations and therapy but looked extremely well that day. Of course, Jason had a favorite story to tell. We sat down at the O'Neill Theater Center "White House" before the ceremony. In addition to mentioning a possible role offered by Hollywood, there was the story of Jason's surgeon. According to "Himself," his surgeon had removed all his Shakespeare, Chekhov, and Shaw, but left untouched his Pinter. With that same mischievous grin, Jason announced, "I was in three Pinter plays and never understood a word of them."

Jason's Monte Cristo Award was presented by Arthur Gelb; it was a small bronze statue by sculptor Norman Legassie of O'Neill as a boy sitting on a rock, "a sketcher of trees and ships." Tears rolled down Jason's cheeks as well as ours. Those tears came once more at the memorial service when James Naughton sang "Danny Boy," a favorite song of Jason's.

"Just Me N'You"

We're outward bound for the land of dreams—
Just me n'you
Our course set by a star that gleams
For me n'you
We've nailed our hope-flag to the mast
Set sail and left behind the Past,
We know we'll reach our port at last—

Just me n'you
Just me n'you
Just you n'me
Till life wake to
Eternity!

Eugene O'Neill
10 January 1915

Christopher Plummer
Remembers

The funeral for Jason Nelson Robards was private. A ceremony and Catholic Mass were held on New Year's Day, 2001. Only Jason's immediate family and closest friends were invited. Jason's widow Lois asked actor Christopher Plummer to give the eulogy. Both have granted the Eugene O'Neill Society permission to publish this text.

There was movement on the station for the word had got around
That the colt from 'Old Regret' had got away.
He had joined the wild bush horses, he was worth a thousand pound
And all the cracks had gathered to the fray.

That was one of Jason's favorites. He never ceased to declaim it at the top of his lungs whenever he entered a restaurant or saloon. It didn't take long before everyone present had forgiven him and was eating out of his hand. And quite mistaking him for the Pied Piper of Hamelin, they would follow him, like children, into the night.

It seems I have known Jason since time began. We started out as young actors working together on Broadway, back in those sunny prehistoric days when there was little difference between the stage and real life—in fact, to Jason they always remained one and the same. He had just come out of the Second World War armed with a big rasping voice, an unholy zest for life and one of the great craggy faces of memory. From the moment I met him I began to smile—and it was-n't long before I was madly trying to emulate his insatiable lust for adventure, only to be carried away by the sudden gusts from that aston-ishing energy of his which was Niagara-like in its intensity. He was Fire and Water—no, that's not quite right—he was Fire, and some-thing a little stronger than water!

The anguish Jason brought to his performances which was so heart-wrenching was not, as might be expected, the anguish of per-sonal pain. Oh no, he loved life and acting far too much to indulge in that sort of nonsense. No, his anguish was born from an almost com-pulsive desire to complete his crusade—namely, to deliver us all of himself, each night—even his very soul, if he could—to give away all his secrets: "He wears his heart upon his sleeve for daws to peck at."

Now we all know that Jason Robards has definitely reincar-nated the spirit of Eugene O'Neill in our time. But he was to do equal justice to many other major writers of plays. I know. I stood on the same stage beside him when he gave the most wonderful performance of Shakespeare's Hotspur I have ever seen. This Hotspur was a coarse warrior whose biggest battle was the battle to express himself, and the agony he went through to find the right words was excruciatingly funny and deeply touching. But when Jason's Hotspur grasped at straws he could recognize and hold onto, the sheer tenacity of his quest for truth and glory freed the poetry in him and when he reached for the sky "to pluck bright honour from the pale-faced moon"—he was unforget-table.

Another memory I have is of the wee hours of many mornings when all the parties were over and we were all lying about in heaps— Jason would take up his guitar and in that charming whisky-baritone he would softly chant—"summers in Bordeaux—rowing a bateau—just a dream ago—when the world was young." He would sing this refrain over and over, bridge and all, as if to some private and misbegotten moon.

What was the secret that lay deep down in Jason's core that made him so entrancing, so original? Was it his great talent that could move storms and summon up dragons? Was it the restless personality that demanded at all times to be larger than life, or was it the young rebel in him he refused to let die? Or was it simply his generous spirit, his sublime sense of fun, his compassion and his fierce loyalty as a friend who would fight to the death for you? Of course it was all of those things but there was something else—something quite intangible, and it's called innocence—yes, that's what it was—he never lost that quality of innocence—you could see it in his eyes. It was innocence that made him vulnerable, that made us laugh and cry at the same time. It was his innocence that helped give Jason his pathos and his magic and that made him so remarkable and so loved as an artist and as a man.

Knowing him, as I have, all these long years, has made me prouder than I could ever dream of being—and—infinitely content. For knowing Jason, just for one day, could make life, with all its peccadillos—suddenly seem very worthwhile.

Margaret and Ralph Ranald Remember

> Margaret Loftus Ranald is Past President of the Eugene O'Neill Society, and author of *The Eugene O'Neill Companion*. Ralph Arthur Ranald teaches literature and the law at CUNY, and at Harvard. They recall their reactions to news of Jason Robards' death and to the memorial ceremony that followed.

When we heard that Jason Robards had died, Ralph and I immediately felt overwhelmed. Partly it was the news itself. But we also, involuntarily, re-experienced our initial reaction to his performances in the first American production of *Long Day's Journey Into Night* (1956) and in *A Moon for the Misbegotten* (1973–1974) which we had seen decades ago. Later, in the eighties, we were able to take our daughter, Caroline, then an undergraduate, to see Robards in a revival of *The Iceman Cometh*, and saw that she was affected as we had been. We visited Robards briefly after the *Iceman* performance and were surprised and filled with pity when we saw how exhausted he seemed.

As we know, Jason Robards, along with the director José Quintero, was at the center of the rediscovery of Eugene O'Neill that began after the playwright's death. The revival began with the first successful productions of the family plays that O'Neill wrote in California after his health began to fail. (Quintero, who also recently died, gave an account of these productions and of Robards' achievements in his autobiography, *If You Don't Dance, They Beat You.*) It seems to us that these performances have never been equalled.

Like everyone, we know of the difficulties Robards experienced with alcoholism and failed marriages. We saw, perhaps, a glimpse of how the difficulties were overcome, when we attended the funeral of Ralph's colleague and friend, the Reverend Timothy Healey, S.J., who died in December 1992. One of those who attended the funeral was Jason Robards, who seemed to be very affected and who gazed at Father Healey's body with what appeared to be a feeling of reverence and very deep mourning. After, Robards told Ralph that Father Healey had helped him in the time of his trouble; Robards seemed to feel he owed Father Healey much for his ability to carry on his work with O'Neill in the seventies and after. We treasure the memory of the brief conversation that day.

A few months ago, Robards came to a ceremony at Monte Cristo Cottage where he was given a small copy of the lifesized statue that stands near the New London railway station, a sculpture depicting the boy Eugene sitting on a rock and reading. I sat near him and could see that, although he was very weak, he was delighted by the gift. Perhaps both Father Healey and Jason Robards are resting together now, but I think of the two together, in life.

The Roundabout Theatre, "Remembering Jason Robards, 1922–2000"

> The following, which was published in the Roundabout Theatre Company's Newsletter, *Front and Center*, in January 2001, is used with the kind permission of the Roundabout.

On Wednesday, December 27, at 7:55, the lights of Broadway bowed low for Jason Robards, who had passed away the previous day at the age of 78. The marquee of the Roundabout's new theatre—which Robards helped to create—was among those darkened at curtain time in acknowledgement of his light and spirit, and as a symbol of our profound regard for his life and work. His guidance and inspiration as a member of Roundabout's Board of Directors was a gift surpassed only by his presence, his warmth, and his friendship. We join the artistic community in mourning the loss of a tireless advocate of the theatre and a great force on the stage.

Although revered as one of America's greatest actors, Robards remained modest and philosophical about his many celebrated accomplishments, and once remarked that "All I know about acting is that I just have to keep on doing it." Robards held the record for Tony Award nominations for Best Actor in a Play, with no fewer than eight nominations testifying to his unequaled talents. Widely acknowledged as the greatest interpreter of Eugene O'Neill's dramas, he was honored by the Kennedy Center in 1999. Future generations will find his performances preserved in an extensive list of film roles, for which he twice received Academy Awards (for *All the President's Men* in 1977 and *Julia* in 1978). But he was steadfast in his commitment to the stage, and once said he would always rather "go back to Broadway as fast as I can."

Following his first Broadway production (*Stalag 17*) in 1951, Robards went on to give many more. His unforgettable performances contributed to some of the most important, moving, and artistically accomplished productions in the American theatre, and were essential to the recognition of many now-classic plays. They include O'Neill's landmark dramas *The Iceman Cometh, Long Day's Journey Into Night, A Moon for the Misbegotten,* and *A Touch of the Poet*; Budd Schulberg's and Harvey Breit's *The Disenchanted* (for which he won a Tony in 1959); Herb Gardner's *A Thousand Clowns*; and Arthur Miller's *After the Fall.*

Of one of his greatest roles, O'Neill's Jamie Tyrone, he said, "He's a tumbleweed. That's what I am. He had no home—just jumping around so much. I find a lot of parallels between us." Of working with us, he has said: "It's like family being at Roundabout. All of us who work there feel that way; it feels like coming home." At Roundabout, Robards performed with his friend Christopher Plummer in the first New York revival of Harold Pinter's *No Man's Land* in 1994. The following season he went on to support the inauguration of our Laura Pels Theatre with his performances in Pinter's *Moonlight* and Brian Friel's *Molly Sweeney.* During that exceptional year, he was known affectionately as our "artist in residence," and everyone from the front door to backstage was blessed with his open and sharing spirit.

Jason Robards, a veteran of six decades on the American stage, once said that "the theatre has kept me alive," and he worked to keep the theatre alive for all of us. We are profoundly grateful for all he did and pause to remember that when he was with us, it was grand.

Charles Saydah,
"Jason Robards, 1922–2000"

Reprinted from *The Bergen* (N.J.) *Record*, December 28, 2000, with the kind permission of the *Record* and Charles Saydah.

There are occasions when life and art become indistinguishable. When the music or the painting or the poetry realigns our conception of reality so that we can't tell the difference between the two—that's as simple a definition of great, everlasting art as can be devised. Over the last half-century, many of the greatest moments of such high art on the American stage occurred whenever Jason Robards played a role from a Eugene O'Neill play.

Sure, Mr. Robards, who died Tuesday at 78, had a rich and varied career in film and television. They're the media in which most people have seen him and by which his abilities will continue to be on display and judged. His odd presence gave a quirky life to a range of characters, famed and obscure—Dashiell Hammett, Al Capone, Howard Hughes; rebellious television writers, bigoted lawyers, crusty old men. He even picked up a couple of Academy Awards for his work.

But it was on the stage in such roles as Hickey from *The Iceman Cometh* and Jamie Tyrone in *Long Day's Journey Into Night* that Mr. Robards—his charming manner, distinctive voice, uncommon intelligence, and his years of hard living—found his true home.

Starting in 1956 with his stunning portrayal of the evangelical

Hickey in José Quintero's revival of *The Iceman Cometh*, Mr. Robards stunned audiences with his scratchy-voiced recitations of O'Neill's ruminations on the recesses of the human spirit. He gave vibrant life to otherwise despairing words and thoughts and characters, converting darkness into light, desolation into hope. By his uncanny connection to the playwright and his work, he made his audiences part of the drama and grafted it onto their lives. The deep inhalations they made whenever Mr. Robards came to the revelatory points of O'Neill's great soliloquies were shocks of personal recognition, not simply reflexive acknowledgments of his acting skills.

Although we will no longer have the privilege of watching Mr. Robards provide such memorable theatrical experiences, we still have the modern miracle of recording. Out in some old record collection— a college library, a garage sale, a discard bin of a public library converting its sound collection from analog to digital—there's a scratchy copy of Mr. Robards reciting O'Neill. Retrieve it. Play it.

It won't be the same as watching Mr. Robards in the flesh. But you'll feel some of the same awe that overwhelmed Mr. Quintero 44 years ago when a 34-year-old actor, destined for a small role in *The Iceman Cometh*, gave an unscheduled audition for the leading part, silencing the director, converting himself into a star, and elevating a clunky, didactic play about a bunch of drunks into its current position as one of the masterpieces of the American stage.

Kevin Spacey, "An Example, a Mentor, an Actor Above All"

> Kevin Spacey played Jamie Tyrone in *Long Day's Journey Into Night* in 1986 in New York, and played Hickey in *The Iceman Cometh* in 1998 in London and New York. The following appeared in *The New York Times*, January 14, 2001, and is reprinted with the kind permission of Mr. Spacey and the *Times*. Copyright © 2001 by the New York Times Company.

It was a cinch for me to make good. I had the knack.
Hickey in The Iceman Cometh

Jason Robards and I were both born on July 26—he in 1922; I in 1959. It was just the beginning of our connection to each other, which goes way beyond the mere coincidence of a shared birth date. He was the first actor to play Jamie Tyrone in Eugene O'Neill's *Long Day's Journey Into Night* on Broadway 45 years ago. I was the second actor to play Jamie on Broadway 15 years ago. He gave enduring life to the character of Hickey in O'Neill's *Iceman Cometh* in 1956. I took on the role of Hickey in *Iceman* in 1998.

I first met Jason in Washington in the fall of 1985, two months before I was to begin *Long Day's Journey*. I was about to start rehearsals in *The Seagull* at the Kennedy Center. It seems only appropriate that the woman playing my mother in that production, and who played so many great performances with Jason, Colleen Dewhurst, would introduce us. The occasion was the closing-night party for the pre–Broadway run of *Iceman*. Jason was playing Hickey again in José Quintero's revival of the O'Neill classic, which had brought them both fame and bound their fates so many years before. I would sneak into the presidential box of the Eisenhower Theater to watch the master, night after night. For a master Hickey he was. I must have seen a dozen performances.

Colleen knew of my admiration for Jason and she told me that she was taking me to the closing party specifically to meet him. I told her that I would be too embarrassed. She told me to shut my mouth and mind my own business. When Colleen Dewhurst told you to shut up, you shut up. So we went. The reception was in the ballroom of the Bristol Hotel on Pennsylvania Avenue, a few blocks from the White House. I sat with Colleen through hors d'oeuvres I did not taste, for my eyes were glued to the great man across the room. I could not help watching Jason. And I sensed that he knew who I was. He kept turning in his seat, looking back toward our table. Our eyes occasionally met. Someone must have pointed me out to him, I thought. I suspected a certain devilish woman whom I called Mother Earth. But then, that was Colleen: bringing people together.

As the evening wound down, Jason got up, said his goodnights and moved through the ballroom on his way out, shaking hands, kissing cheeks, all the while heading in our direction. I sat frozen in my chair as I sensed him coming up behind us. I felt the hair on my neck rise. Then I felt a hand on my shoulder. I looked up and Jason was staring down at me with that miraculous face of his. He smiled and said: "Be good to him. He was very good to me." I knew instantly that he was talking about Jamie. I knew he was wishing me well in the part. In that moment I felt a kinship with Jason that never wavered.

I am greatly sad at his passing. I have felt relief that he is at last free of the long and difficult struggle he waged over his health. But I can't ignore my selfish desire that he stick around forever. I want to hear that distinctive voice telling me his opinions: on the news, politics, the state of the theater, movies, the Screen Actors' strike. At 78, he was still driven by concern for his fellow actors. He remained interested and curious about almost everything. He could be a great talker, that's true. But he was an even better listener. And he listened to no one with a more open heart than the voice of a playwright.

It is curious that he never met the playwright who made him famous. But I can imagine a few drunken nights they might have shared together. The first play he read of O'Neill's was *Strange Interlude* aboard ship during his stint in the Navy. How fitting that O'Neill and Robards would meet at sea.

What was it about Jason? To pursue the meaning of a man's existence has always seemed to me absurd. The most beautiful experiences we can have are the mysterious. Yet everyone has certain measurements by which they judge a man's endeavors. Mine are those of an actor.

Actors loved Jason Robards because we know what it takes. Every actor strives to achieve what Jason accomplished so effortlessly, or seemingly so. He worked hard, make no mistake, but he was such a superb technician that he managed to make us forget that he was working at all. I think Jason was also in on his own joke. He had no patience for the self-analysis that some indulged in. He was not interested in the psychology of acting. His view of acting was just do it. Learn it. Serve it. Jason didn't spend his time trying to figure it all out. He was too busy working. Not taking it all too seriously.

It is this prevailing attitude—which is conducive to a view of life—that gives humor its place. I think this is one of the major reasons that Jason, while an accomplished dramatic actor, was also able to develop his keen comic ability. He could be very funny: watch *A Thousand Clowns*. And that laugh of his; contagious, crackling and rapid-fire.

Seeing Jason on stage and screen, you marveled when he reached for a moment and grabbed it. Watch the scope of his anguish in *Long Day's Journey* opposite Katharine Hepburn; his authority and intelligence as Ben Bradlee in *All the President's Men*; his moving romantic turn as Dashiell Hammett with Jane Fonda in *Julia*; and his amazing transformation as Howard Hughes in *Melvin and Howard*. We are also fortunate to have on film and tape Jason's work onstage in *The Iceman Cometh* and *A Moon for the Misbegotten*, two of his most searing performances.

Actors know a great performance when they see one because inside every actor is a great performance. A thousand things come between most actors and their dreams. There are only a handful, like Jason, who are given the chance, and have the courage, to give audiences the best and the worst of themselves. Again and again. So actors live through a performer like Jason Robards. He was brave. He adored the craft of acting; he clung to it and honored it. Actors can tell the difference between those who respect the written word and serve the material and those who set out to serve themselves. Jason fought to be the best because, in some measure, he recognized what he meant to the acting community—how we responded to his work and career.

His passing is significant because, with few exceptions, he is the last of a breed of actors of his stature who dedicated themselves to a life in the theater. We never had to witness his systematic corruption by success. He had an unerring sense of the right thing to do: he acted in the interest of the profession and, without asking for the role, he was our elder statesman. He held the bar high for others, but even higher for himself. Because of that, every actor wants a career like that of Jason Robards.

Without the friendship of those of like mind, the struggle for the eternally unattainable in the arts would seem empty. Actors bond together; that's our nature. But with Jason it was more than that. I could say he was more than a mentor. He became something of another father to me.

A year ago, Jason and I were back in Washington. I was presenting the tribute to him for the Kennedy Center Honors. I felt privileged to be able to pay homage to his work in such a public way. Just before last Thanksgiving, a month before he died, he drove into Manhattan to return the favor. At the Plaza Hotel he presented me with an award from the Actor's Fund for my work in the theater. He said things that night that I wish I could have heard my own father say. My father didn't live long enough to see me play Hickey in *Iceman*. But Jason came. Eight years ago my father died the day before Christmas. And now Jason, the day after.

For those who still believe in the magic of storytelling, Jason Robards's passionate commitment to the art of acting will burn so bright that the lights of the American theater will never go out.

Eli Wallach Remembers

Eli Wallach won the Tony Award for *The Rose Tattoo* (1951) and was in numerous plays including *Camino Real* (1953), *The Waltz of the Toreadors* (1973), and *Visiting Mr. Green* (1997). These remarks were given at the public memorial service at the Broadhurst Theatre in New York.

Some forty years ago, Jason and I appeared in a live TV drama—I played my usual Mexican bandit, Jason was an American engineer—and we engaged in a volatile verbal duel. Suddenly, he stopped, drained of color, and appeared about to faint. Poor man, I thought, he'll never make it in this profession—because he gets faint when he becomes emotional ... little did I know!

Last night I had a vivid dream. I was Sancho Panza—sitting on my little gray ass—and beside me, astride a white, sway-backed mare, sat a gangly, skinny man, strangely dressed. He wore dented armor—he wore, not a helmet, but a Viennese hat—and instead of a lance, he carried a ukulele. He was muttering phrases like "Impossible dream" or fight "the unfightable foe." "Vamonos," he cried—and, strumming his ukulele, he sang, "Swanee, how I miss you, my dear old Swanee." Riding along, we crossed a desert. "Sire," I said, "I'm exhausted and very hot." "It's all right, kid," he replied, "don't worry, *The Iceman Cometh*." On we rode. "Sire," I cried, "look at the Moon." "Oh yes," he said, "the damn Moon is full, but not Misbegotten." I heard a train whistle in the distance—"Hughie-a-Hughie; Clickety-clack."

Jason Robards at the grave of Blemie, O'Neill's dalmatian, at the Tao House property. Used by the kind permission of the Eugene O'Neill Foundation–Tao House.

Finally we reached a theatre—a lot of broads standing about. It was the *Broad*hurst Theatre. We were escorted to the rear of the orchestra by a Spanish-speaking usher named Quintero. He handed us two copies of the *New York Times*. "Sire," I said, "You have a page-and-a-half obit!" "Oh sure," he grumbled, "just a rehashing of old shows, just reopenings of old wounds!" "But sire," I said, "you have a paragraph on the editorial page!" "Oh yes," he muttered, "that's unique for New York. Can you say Unique, New York, five times rapidly?" I tried, but failed. "Ask your audience to say Unique, New York, five times fast!"— they tried and couldn't.

"Sire," I said, "there is a tremendous turnout in this theatre. Every seat is filled. When I go, they'll only be half a house." My sire smiled and said, "Don't worry, kid—we'll paper the house!" "I'm despondent, despairing, and unhappy," I cried. "I know, I know," sighed my patron—he patted my head and continued—"I know, I know—it's been a *Long Day's Journey Into Night!*" To cheer me up, he shouted "Send in the Clowns"—and a Thousand Clowns came onstage—and began to sing an old Negro spiritual: "Going Home, we're going Home."

I awoke with a start—sitting in my kitchen on Riverside Drive—and the window was open. I could still hear the Thousand Clown chorus singing, "We Love You, Jason. We love you, we love you, we love you."

Appendix: Jason Robards' Performances in Theatre, Film and Television

THEATRE

1949   *The Petrified Forest*

1951   *Stalag 17*

1952   *The Chase*

1954   *American Gothic*

1956   *The Iceman Cometh*
         Long Day's Journey Into Night

1958   *The Disenchanted*
         Henry IV, Part I
         The Winter's Tale

1959   *Macbeth*

1960   *Toys in the Attic*

1961   *Big Fish, Little Fish*

1962   *A Thousand Clowns*

1964   *Hughie*
         But for Whom, Charlie
         After the Fall

1965   *The Devils*

1968   *We Bombed in New Haven*

1972   *The Country Girl*

1973   *A Moon for the Misbegotten*

1976   *That Championship Season*
        Hughie
        Long Day's Journey Into Night

1977   *A Touch of the Poet*

1983   *You Can't Take It with You*

1985   *The Iceman Cometh*

1987   *A Month of Sundays*

1988   *Long Day's Journey Into Night*
        Ah, Wilderness!

1989   *Love Letters*

1991   *Park Your Car in Harvard Yard*

1994   *No Man's Land*

1996   *Moonlight*

1997   *Molly Sweeney*

FILM

1959   *The Journey*

1961   *By Love Possessed*

1962   *Tender Is the Night*
        Long Day's Journey Into Night

1963   *Act One*

1965   *A Thousand Clowns*

1966   *A Big Hand for the Little Lady*
        Any Wednesday

1967   *Divorce American Style*
        Hour of the Gun
        The St. Valentine's Day Massacre

1968   *Isadora*
        The Night They Raided Minsky's

1969   *Once Upon a Time in the West*

1970   *Julius Caesar*
       The Ballad of Cable Hogue
       Tora! Tora! Tora!
       Fools
       Operation Snafu

1971   *Johnny Got His Gun*
       Murders in the Rue Morgue

1972   *The War Between Men and Women*
       Death of a Stranger

1973   *Pat Garrett and Billy the Kid*

1975   *Mr. Sycamore*
       A Boy and His Dog

1976   *All the President's Men*

1977   *Julia*

1978   *Comes a Horseman*

1979   *Hurricane*
       Melvin and Howard
       Raise the Titanic

1981   *Capoblanco*
       The Legend of the Lone Ranger

1983   *Max Dugan Returns*
       Something Wicked This Way Comes

1987   *Square Dance*

1988   *Bright Lights, Big City*
       The Good Mother

1989   *Dream a Little Dream*
       Parenthood
       Reunion

1991   *Black Rainbow*
       Quick Change

1992   *Storyville*

1993   *The Adventures of Huckleberry Finn*
       Philadelphia
       The Trial

1994   *Little Big League*
       The Paper

1996   *Crimson Tide*
       The Real McCaw

1997   *A Thousand Acres*
       Beloved

1998   *Enemy of the State*

2000   *Magnolia*

SELECTED TELEVISION

1956   Playhouse 90 / *For Whom the Bell Tolls*

1960   *The Iceman Cometh*

1963   *One Day in the Life of Ivan Denisovitch*

1967   *Noon Wine*

1972   *The House Without
       A Christmas Tree*

1973   *The Country Girl*

1977   *Washington: Behind Closed Doors*

1978   *A Christmas to Remember*

1980   *F.D.R.: The Last Years*
       Haywire

1981   *Hughie*

1983   *The Day After*

1984   *Sakharov*

1985   *The Atlanta Child Murders*
       The Long Hot Summer

1986   *Johnny Bull*
       The Last Frontier

1987   *Laguna Heat*
       *Norman Rockwell's Breaking
       Home Ties*

1988   *The Christmas Wife*
       Inherit the Wind

1991 *The Perfect Tribute*
   An Inconvenient Woman
   Mark Twain and Me
   Chernobyl: The Final Warning

1993 *Heidi*

1994 *The Enemy Within*

1995 *My Ántonia*

1996 *Journey*

1999 *Going Home*

Index

Abbey Theatre 106
Academy Awards (Oscars) 126, 160, 188, 189
Academy Festival Theatre (Chicago) 139
Actors Studio 51, 82
After the Fall 56, 125, 188
Ah! Wilderness 9, 21, 24, 70, 104, 109*n1*, 114, 115, 120, 125, 143, 180
Albertoni, Kaye Radovan 129
Alexander, Doris 108
All God's Chillun Got Wings 110*n4*, 115
All the President's Men 108, 138–139, 177, 188, 193
American Academy of Dramatic Arts 9, 11, 28, 32, 34, 53, 57, 148
American Gothic 28, 52, 95, 171, 174
Ancestral Voices 162
Anderson, Paul Thomas 12, 177
"Anna Christie" 14, 105, 110*n4*, 115
ANT (American National Theatre) 94, 96, 97, 99
Arturo Ui 148
Atkinson, Brooks 31, 104, 105, 166–167

Bacall, Lauren 64, 138
Backe, Gloria Scott 27
Bains, Conrad 18
The Ballad of Cable Hogue 56, 177
Barnes, Clive 73, 101
Barrymore, John 56
Barrymore, Maurice 81
Barton, James 9, 23, 28, 57, 167
Bates, Kathy 16

Beecroft, George 119–121
Bentley, Eric 21
Berliner Ensemble 113
Berne, Gustave 36
Beverly Hills 138
Beyond the Horizon 63, 74
Big Fish, Little Fish 159
Billingsley, Sherman 119
The Birth of Tragedy 41
Black, Stephen A. 26*n2*, 114, 155
Blackburn, Clarice 171
Blair, Bill 135
Blair, Darlene 135, 137, 139, 140
Blemie (Silverdene Emblem) 114, 116*n4*, 196
Boatwright, Daniel E. 126
Bogard, Travis 2, 8, 20, 41, 72, 75–76, 122–128, 123, 135, 136, 140, 143
Booth, Edwin 56, 67
Booth, John Wilkes 67
Booth, Junius Brutus 67
Boulton, Agnes 107, 119–121
Bound East for Cardiff 110*n4*
Bowen, Croswell 107
Brando, Marlon 56
Brecht Bertolt 113
Breit, Harvey 188
Brietzke, Zander 112–116
Bristol Hotel 192
Broderick, Matthew 13, 115
Brooks, Patricia 27
Brown, Arvin 106, 109*n1*, 114, 129–130
Brown Derby 174
Bryer, Jackson R. 107

Burns, Ric 116*n*6, 168
Bush, George 126, 143
Butch Cassidy and the Sundance Kid 148
"By Way of Obit" 36
Byrne, Gabriel 25
Byron, Lord 83, 87

Caldwell, Zoe 22, 71, 131–132, 180
Campbell, Douglas 133
Cargill, Oscar 107
The Carol Burnett Show 89
Carradine, John 174
Charleson, Ian 149–150
The Chase 125
Chekhov, Anton 101, 113, 124, 181
Chelsea Hotel 154
Circle in the Square 37, 38, 53, 82, 95,
   98, 166–167; catalyst for Off–Broad-
   way movement 96, 113, 171; lack of
   offstage space 8; 1956 description of
   96; 1956 revival of *The Iceman
   Cometh* 1, 27–31, 51, 94, 96, 97, 98,
   113, 119–121, 125, 172
Clurman, Harold 82, 87, 105, 106
The Cocktail Hour 161
Cohan, George M. 70
Commons, Thomas 41
Connecticut College 180
Connell, Leigh 30
Contour in Time 140
Cooper, Wendy 134–143
Cotter, Sean 72, 76
The Count of Monte Cristo 33
The Country Girl 56, 159–160, 163
Cranston, Alan 126, 143
Cronyn, Hume 159
Curran Theatre (San Francisco) 37
The Curse of the Misbegotten 107
Cusack, Cyril 106

Danner, Blythe 144–145, 148
Danville (California) 114, 138
Darnton, John 168
da Silva, Howard 28
Davison, Richard Allan 146–150
The Day After 125
The Day of the Dolphin 60
Days Without End 24
Dellums, Ron 126
Desire Under the Elms 70, 105, 106,
   109*n*2, 110*n*4, 115

Dewhurst, Colleen 9, 13, 22, 55, 57,
   63, 71, 73, 74–77, 82, 106, 112, 113,
   115, 124, 128, 144, 148, 156, 161, 166,
   191–192
di Cori, Ferruccio 60, 67
Diff'rent 106
Dillman, Bradford 34, 35, 50
Dionysus 41–42, 44–45
The Disenchanted 56, 109, 146–147, 155,
   158, 188
Dodson, Jack 8, 11, 37, 135–141
Dodson, Mary 140
Donnelly, H. R. 78–79
Dorman, Craig 140
Dowling, Vincent 76
Drake, Sylvie 137

Eaton, Richard 103–111
The Ed Sullivan Show 158
Eder, Richard 88
Edinburgh Festival 107
Edwards, Ben 96, 101
Einenkel, Robert 151–152
Eisenhower Theatre (Washington,
   D.C.) 97, 192
Eldridge, Florence 34, 35, 50
Elliott, Denholm 89, 91
Emmys 108–109, 160
The Emperor Jones 110*n*4
The Entertainer 147
Erickson, Mitch 86, 87
Erstein, Hap 97
Eugene O'Neill and the American Critic
   107
Eugene O'Neill Festival 114
Eugene O'Neill Foundation–Tao
   House 2, 122, 134, 135, 138, 142–143
Eugene O'Neill National Historic Site
   140
The Eugene O'Neill Review 2
Eugene O'Neill Society 1–4, 72, 103,
   154, 155
Eugene O'Neill Theater Center 13,
   114, 126, 143, 169, 181

Fagin, N. Bryllion 107
Fagles, Robert 149
Falk, Doris 107
Falk, Peter 27, 31, 98
Feingold, Michael 86
Fergusson, Francis 69

Ferrer, José 105
Fields, W. C. 89
Film Critics' Circle Award 126
Fisher, William J. 107
Fitzgerald, F. Scott 56, 146, 148
Fitzgerald, Geraldine 71, 86, 106
Fitzgerald, Zelda 146
Flanders, Ed 63, 71, 73, 82, 112
Floyd, Virginia 26*n*2, 41
Fonda, Henry 78
Fonda, Jane 106, 193
For Whom the Bell Tolls 60
Ford, Gerald 140
Fordham University 105
Frankenheimer, John 23, 60, 79
Fridshtein, I. G. 110*n*5
Friel, Brian 188

Gabel, Martin 159
Gallagher, Peter 143
García Lorca, Federico 166
Gardner, Herb 188
Garvey, Sheila Hickey 27–39, 93–102, 153–157
Gassner, John 108
Gazzara, Ben 106
Geary Theatre (San Francisco) 8
Gelb, Arthur 6, 20, 24, 33, 49–53, 107, 109, 110*n*6, 114, 126, 143, 168, 180, 181
Gelb, Barbara 6, 20, 24, 54–67, 79, 82, 83, 107, 109, 110*n*6, 114, 126, 143, 168, 180
Gentile, Al 138–139
Gideon 147
Gielgud, John 159
Gilpin, Charles 68, 125, 126, 135
"A Glory of Ghosts" 76
Gold 110*n*4
Gottfried, Martin 86
The Grass Harp 27
The Great God Brown 22, 24, 106
Greene, James 27, 28, 94, 95, 97, 98, 99, 100, 101
Greenwich Village 52, 120, 166
Grizzard, George 12, 115, 148, 158–160
Gurney, A. R. 161–162
Gussow, Mel 113

The Hairy Ape 110*n*4, 115
Hall, Peter 109*n*2
Halleburton, Isabelle 172

Hallmark Hall of Fame 163
Hamlet 69, 77, 150
Harris, Barbara 148
Harris, Leonard 86
Harris, Rosemary 146
Harvard University 164
Hawkins, Jack 62
Hayes, Helen 16, 82, 106
Hays, David 36, 96, 156
Healey, Father Timothy 186
Helen Hayes Theatre 51, 82
Hell Hole (Golden Swan) 119
Hellman, Lillian 56, 125
Hemingway, Ernest 148
Henry, Buck 60
Hepburn, Katharine 106, 126, 143
Heston, Charlton 106
Hiller, Wendy 106
Hingle, Pat 106
Holbrook, Hal 106
Holder, Geoffrey 164
Hollywood 139
Hollywood High School 52
Holm, Celeste 105
Homer 148
Houseman, John 159
Hughie 8, 11, 13, 22, 24, 66, 70, 72, 73, 90, 94, 103, 106, 109, 109*n*1, 110*n*4, 113, 125, 132, 154, 156, 167, 174, 180; benefit performance (1975) 135, 136–138; 1964 production 35–38
Humphreys, Dave and Marj 135
Huntington Hartford Theatre (Los Angeles) 37
Huston, Walter 29, 68

The Iceman Cometh 13, 21, 132; comparison of Hickey to Erie Smith 36; English productions 110*n*4; entrance of Hickey 101; Frankenheimer film 23, 59–60, 65–66, 79; Hickey as forerunner of Willy Loman 124; humor in 9, 19; madness of Hickey 83; musical structure 41; 1946 production 4, 23, 31, 57, 72, 105, 125; 1956 revival at Circle in the Square 1, 22–25, 27–32, 51, 54–55, 68, 71, 72, 73, 94, 97–99, 104–106, 108, 113, 119–121, 125, 135, 172, 174–175, 190, 191; 1960 television production 22, 40, 42–48, 108, 193; 1985 revival at

Kennedy Center 93–102, 113, 191–192; 1985 transfer to Broadway 22, 66, 101, 140, 185; 1998 production with Kevin Spacey 191, 194; at O'Neill's 100th Birthday party 167; requires fine acting 77; Robards' interpretation 17–21, 90, 142, 180, 188; Robards performs monologue from 12; staple of O'Neill repertory 115; theme of alcoholism 99–100; use of Nietzschean myth 41–42
If You Don't Dance, They Beat You 186
Ile 110*n4*
In the Zone 110*n4*
Inadmissable Evidence 147
An Inconvenient Woman 143
Inherit the Wind 125
Ivey, Judith 115, 147

Jackson, Anne 18, 115, 126, 142
Jehlinger, Charles 32
Jones, Carol Lea 142
Jones, James Earl 106
Jones, Robert Edmond 81
Julia 108, 177, 188, 193

Kalem, T. E. 73, 86, 91
Kathzka, Gabriel 36
Kauffmann, Stanley 88–90
Kaufmann, Walter 41
Keach, Stacy 106
Kennedy Center 63, 93, 94, 159
Kennedy Center Honors 160, 188, 194
Kerr, Walter 31, 73, 88–90
King, Archer 104–105
King John 147
King Lear 48, 154
Klein, Alvin, 101
Knight, Shirley 163
Korman, Harvey 89
Kroll, Jack 86
Krutch, Joseph Wood 69

Lambs Club 154
Langner, Lawrence 81
Lansing, Robert 106
Larner, Daniel 164–165
Laura Pels Theatre 188
Lazarus Laughed 105
Leech, Clifford 108
Legassie, Norman 181

Lemmon, Jack 106, 126, 143
Levine, Joseph E. 36
Libin, Paul 166–168
Lincoln Center Repertory Company 35
Lindsay, Howard 56
Lithgow, John 106
Long Day's Journey Into Night 9, 11, 12, 13, 16, 21, 30, 36, 65, 67, 77, 90, 103, 104, 108, 109, 125, 126, 131, 132, 135, 143, 156, 169, 172, 176, 177, 180, 185, 188, 191; international productions 106–107, 110*n4*; 1956 production 32–35, 49–52, 55, 56, 58, 64, 71, 72, 73, 106, 108, 113, 149, 151–152, 174; 1962 film 108, 126, 193; 1988 production 22, 66, 109*n1*, 113, 143; Olivier television production 26*n2*; world premiere in Sweden 109*n2*
The Long Voyage Home 105, 106
Los Angeles Times 137
Love Letters 161–162
The Lower Depths 9
Lumet, Sidney 22, 25, 40, 42, 46
Lunt, Alfred 5, 147
Lunt-Fontanne Theatre 101, 140
Lyons, Jeffrey 101

Macbeth 69, 125
MacGowran, Jack 36
Magnolia 10, 12, 148, 177
Malden, Karl 105
Manheim, Michael 22–26
Mann, Ted (Theodore) 13, 22, 23, 24, 26*n2*, 27, 29, 30, 31, 35, 36, 106, 125, 166, 167, 171–175
March, Fredric 10, 11, 13, 34, 35, 50, 52, 53, 71, 147
Marco Millions 106
Marshall, E. G. 28
Martin, Elliot 82, 87, 89, 91
Marvin, Lee 23, 59–60, 65, 79, 106
Matthau, Walter 138
May, Henry 136
Mayo Clinic 12, 15, 100
McCarthy, Kevin 105
McCormick, Myron 18
McCusker, Stella 76
McDonald, Lois 169–170
McDonough, Edwin 81–92, 104
McKenna, Siobhan 76

McNamara, Dermot 82, 84, 86
McQueen, Steve 8
McQuoid, Jack 76
Melvin and Howard 108, 176, 178, 193
Meredith, Burgess 36
Mermaid Theatre 106
Merola, Deborah 15-21
Miller, Arthur 56, 69, 124, 125, 188
Miller, Betty 90
Miller, George 126, 143
Miller, Jonathan 106
Miller, Jordan 107
Mitchell, Thomas 147
Molière 113
Molly Sweeney 188
Monte Cristo Cottage (Connecticut)
114, 169, 170, 179, 180, 186
Monte Cristo Cottage Award 169,
180-181, 186
Monterey, Carlotta (Mrs. Eugene
O'Neill) 8, 27, 36, 153, 156
A Moon for the Misbegotten 22, 24–25,
42, 53, 105, 106, 107, 109, 109*n2*,
110*n4*, 113, 125, 132, 180; 1947 pro-
duction 81, 105, 125; 1957 production
106; 1973 production 54–57, 59,
63–66, 72–80, 82, 90, 94, 99, 103,
115, 144, 156, 185, 188; 1975 televised
production 108, 112, 193
Moonlight 144, 148, 188
More Stately Mansions 107, 110*n4*
Morgenstern, Joe 176–178
Morosco Theatre 63, 73, 76, 79–80
Moscow Art Theatre 113
Mourning Becomes Electra 69–70,
109*n2*, 110*n4*, 115
Music Box Theatre 145

Nadel, Norman 37
Nathan, George Jean 81
National Medal of Arts 160
National Park Service 114
National Theatre (London) 150
Naughton, James 115, 181
Neeson, Liam 14, 106
New London (Connecticut) 169, 173,
186
New York Herald Tribune 31
New York Post 37, 101
New York Times 31, 37, 167–168
New York World-Telegram and Sun 37

Newman, Paul 148
Nichols, Mike 60
Nietzsche, Friedrich 41–42, 44
'night, Mother 16
The Night of the Iguana 167
No Man's Land 149, 188
Nobel Prize 83
Norton, Elliot 88

Oakland Tribune 137
Oberlin, Russell 164
Obie Award 126, 160
O'Callaghan, Liam 76
Odets, Clifford 56
The Odyssey 149
Oedipus at Colonus 48
Olivier, Laurence 26*n2*, 67, 81, 91, 106,
147
O'Neill (Gelb) 107, 110*n6*
O'Neill, Ella 24, 65, 74, 170
O'Neill, Eugene: on actors 125; association with Robards and Quintero
38, 101–102, 125; on belief in Furies
54; *Beyond the Horizon* 63, 74; birthplace on Broadway 174; boyhood
home 170; Catholicism 59; conference on 13; delays production of *A
Touch of the Poet* 81; description of
Hickey 23, 29, 99, 113; description of
Monte Cristo Award sculpture 181,
186; as Dionysian playwright 48;
documentary on 115, 168; engraved
face on Tao House Award 127, 134;
excerpts from *Iceman* at Mayo Clinic
15; family dynamic 170; family
plagued by alcoholism 55, 58, 72;
foremost American playwright 68,
123–125; gives first performance
rights to Royal Dramatic Theatre
109*n2*; hated by Eric Bentley 21; at
the Hell Hole in New York 119;
Hoosier hayseeds in *Iceman* 79–80;
The Iceman Cometh 93, 98, 99, 100,
166–167; idea for O'Neill repertory
theatre 114–115; importance of stage
directions 3–4, 19, 75, 83, 142;
influence of elder brother on late
plays 24–25; international productions 106–107; "Just Me N'You" 181;
love/hate in *Long Day's Journey*
77–78; *A Moon for the Misbegotten*

73, 75–78; on musical structure in *The Iceman Cometh* 41; on Nietzschean myth in *Iceman* 41–42; Nobel Prize 83; 100th birthday celebration 167; popularity in Ireland 76; read and seen by Robards 4; recovery from alcoholism 58; revival of public reputation 1, 57–58, 94, 106, 107–108, 125, 185; Robards' affinity for 12–13, 66–71, 115, 125, 138, 141–143, 155–156, 161, 168, 172, 179–180, 188, 189, 191–193; Robards and Quintero as ideal interpreters 113, 115; Robards' opinion of *A Touch of the Poet* 82; on role of Con Melody 81, 86; scholarship about 107–108; sculpture of artist as little boy 173; on suffering as theme of tragedy 44–45; Tao House 134

O'Neill, James 21, 63, 71, 74, 80, 81, 86, 90, 170

O'Neill, James, Jr. 23–25, 58, 64–65, 90, 170

O'Neill, Shane 119

O'Neill: Son and Artist 110n6

O'Neill: Son and Playwright 107, 110n6

O'Shea, Milo 84, 86

O'Toole, Peter 64, 72

Pacino, Al 106

Page, Geraldine 31, 82, 106, 113, 166, 171

Palais Royal Theatre 113

Papp, Joe 126, 142

Parenthood 125

Park Your Car in Harvard Yard 146, 147

Part of a Long Story 107

Pavetti, Sally 169–170, 179–181

Peckinpah, Sam 56, 177

Pelly, Farrell 27, 82, 172

Penn, Leo 71

Petherbridge, Edward 7

Phoenix Theatre 106

Pinter, Harold 148, 181, 188

Playbill 147, 149

Players Club 56, 154, 160

Plaza Hotel 194

Plummer, Christopher 64, 84, 147, 148, 149, 182–184, 188

Point Pleasant (New Jersey) 119

Portman, Eric 82, 84, 89, 91

Powell, Addison 32

Presidential Citation 126

Princeton University 149

Provincetown Playhouse 105, 115

Pulitzer Prize 74

Quayle, Anthony 106

Quilley, Dennis 26n2

Quinn, Anthony 56

Quintero, José 11, 12, 13, 21, 22, 23, 24, 25, 32, 52, 53, 57, 66, 79, 95, 104, 109n1, 156, 166, 175, 180; directing approach 104; directs 1956 revival of *The Iceman Cometh* 1, 23–25, 27–31, 52, 97–98, 104–105, 125, 170, 190; directs 1964 production of *Hughie* 35–38, 106, 167; directs 1973 production of *A Moon for the Misbegotten* 55, 59, 63, 73, 76–77; directs 1977 production of *A Touch of the Poet* 82–91; directs 1985 production of *Iceman* in Washington, D. C. 93–102; directs *American Gothic* 171–172; directs *Desire Under the Elms, Strange Interlude,* and *Marco Millions* 106; directs Robards in *Macbeth* 164–165; on drinking 63, 94, 98, 100; finds humor in O'Neill 9; foremost interpreter of O'Neill 113, 115, 185–186; lunches with Robards and Carlotta Monterey 8; memorial service for 7; named to Theatre Hall of Fame 101; offers Hickey to Robards 9, 26n2; speaking about O'Neill 3

Raleigh, John Henry 108

Ranald, Margaret 185–186

Ranald, Ralph 185–186

Redgrave, Vanessa 106

Richardson, Lee 171

Richardson, Natasha 14, 106

Richardson, Ralph 71, 79, 106

Robards, David 64, 160

Robards, Eleanore 28, 32, 35, 58, 64

Robards, Glenn 60

Robards, Hope 65

Robards, Jake O'Neill 10, 138, 160

Robards, Jason, Jr.: CAREER ACHIEVEMENTS AND LEGACY: 114, 125–126, 187–190, 192–194; association with

Eugene O'Neill Society 1, 3, 180; awards 160; foremost O'Neillian actor 56, 66–71, 115, 138, 169, 180, 183, 188; honored at 2000 O'Neill Conference with Monte Cristo Cottage Award 13–14, 169, 180–181, 186; memorial service 115, 168; Oscar Awards 108; reinvigorates O'Neill's reputation 103–104, 106, 109, 185–186; Tao House prize for Contribution to American Drama 2, 124–127, 134–135, 140–142; television and film credits 108, 189, 199–203; Tony Award 109; Tony nominations 109, 187; O'NEILL PERFORMANCES: 1, 90, 103, 106, 113, 125, 132, 180, 188, 189, 191; description of Robards as Hickey (1956) 172; Hickey (1985) 94–102; as Hickey in *The Iceman Cometh* 192; in *Hughie* (1964) 35–38, 106; *The Iceman Cometh* (1956) 8, 30–32, 97–98, 104, 119–121, 166–167; as Jamie in *Long Day's Journey Into Night* (1956) 32–35, 49–53, 149, 151–152, 167, 174; *A Moon for the Misbegotten* (1973) 54–67, 72–80, 115; *A Moon for the Misbegotten* on television (1975) 112; reading from *Long Day's Journey Into Night* 172; recalls California production of *Hughie* (1975) 8, 136–139; on television in *The Iceman Cometh* (1960) 40–48; *A Touch of the Poet* (1977) 81–91; OTHER PERFORMANCES: *American Gothic* 171–172; *The Country Girl* 159; *The Disenchanted* (1958) 146–147, 158–159; diverse characterizations 148; in film 176–178; as Hotspur 133, 183; *Love Letters* 161; *Macbeth* (1958) 164–165; *Magnolia* 177–178; at the Roundabout Theatre 187–188; *A Thousand Clowns* 148–149, 193; ON ACTING: audition for Hickey 26*n*2, 28–29, 95, 104–106, 113, 174–175; as comedian 193; fellow actors comment about Robards 148; humor in O'Neill 9; interprets *The Iceman Cometh* 17–21, 22–25; interprets Jamie in *Long Day's Journey Into Night* 22–25, 188; interprets Jim Tyrone in *A Moon for the Misbegotten*

24–25; introduction to acting and O'Neill 4, 57, 179; learns by watching Fredric March 11; on the Method and acting O'Neill 12–13, 141–142, 161; outstanding memory helps to play O'Neill roles 9–10; preparing to play Hickey 3–4; in rehearsal 128, 130; vocal qualities 69–70, 133, 148, 172, 177; on work of fellow actors 147–148, 150; writes out entire script of *A Touch of the Poet* 10; PHOTO-GRAPHS: at Blemie's grave at Tao House 196; with Colleen Dewhurst in *A Moon for the Misbegotten* (1974) 73; with Eugene O'Neill Society at MLA Convention 155; with Jack Dodson 136, 137, 141; as Jamie in *Long Day's Journey Into Night* (1956) 50; with Jane Caldwell Washburn 129; with Kaye Radovan Albertoni 129; receiving Monte Cristo Cottage Award 173; speaking at Connecticut College 6; at Tao House (1986) 162; with Travis Bogard at Tao House 123; with Zoe Caldwell 131; PER-SONAL: affinity for music of O'Neill's time 10; attends Father Healey's funeral 186; on automobile accident 58–62, 79; closeness to O'Neill's characters 155–156; death of 2, 113, 187; on drinking 58–59, 63, 66, 72, 78–79, 100, 158–160, 174, 177–178; meets Carlotta Monterey 8; at O'Neill's 100th birthday party 167; physical description (1973) 59, 182–183; private O'Neill collection 156; qualities 182–184, 192–194; relationship with mother 65; relationship to Travis Bogard 136; relationship with his father 10–11, 33–35, 53, 55–56, 90–91, 148, 155, 174; as a storyteller 2, 3–4, 153–157, 179, 181; visits to Monte Cristo Cottage 169–170, 180–181; works with Mayo Clinic to treat alcoholism 11–12, 15–16
Robards, Jason, Sr. 33–35, 49, 53, 55, 57, 63–64, 148, 153, 155, 156, 174
Robards, Jason, III 51, 64, 160, 161
Robards, Lois O'Connor 10, 59–62, 64–66, 79, 127, 135, 137, 138, 140, 153, 154, 156, 160, 180

Robards, Rachel 64
Robards, Sam 16, 64, 115, 160
Robards, Sarah 51, 64, 160
Robards, Shannon 62, 66, 79, 138, 160
Rockwell, Norman 171
The Rope 110*n4*
The Roundabout Theatre 144, 187–188
Ross, Katharine 148
Royal Dramatic Theatre (Stockholm) 36, 109*n2*
Royale Theatre 36, 37
Runyon, Tom 61
Ryan, Robert 106

Sardi's 51
Saydah, Charles 189–190
Schulberg, Budd 158, 188
Scott, George C. 56, 60, 64, 82, 83, 106, 148, 166
Sellars, Peter 95, 99, 100
Shafer, Yvonne 7–14
Shakespeare 53, 67, 101, 113, 115, 124, 133, 148, 164, 181, 183
Shaughnessy, Edward L. 68–80
Shaw, George Bernard 181
Sheaffer, Louis 20, 24, 107, 109, 110*n6*
Sheridan Square 8, 28, 96, 166, 171
Simon, John 86
Sizoo, Lois 135, 138, 139, 140
Sizoo, Wes 135
Skelton, Thomas R. 101
Skinner, Richard Dana 107
Skorodenkoed, V. A. 110*n5*
Smith, Madeline 103–111
Snider, Barry 85
Spacey, Kevin 13, 71–72, 115, 191–194
Spoleto Festival 36, 106
S. S. Glencairn 105
Stalag 17 8, 51, 125, 174, 188
Stanley, Kim 82, 106
Stapleton, Maureen 148, 159
Stasio, Marilyn 85
Stevens, Roger 94
Stevens, Sydney 166
Stork Club 119
Strange Interlude 4, 7, 57, 70, 106, 126, 179, 193
Strasberg, Lee 12, 91
Stratford Shakespeare Festival 147, 148, 154–155
Stritch, Elaine 161

Suffolk University 3
Summer and Smoke 31, 113, 171

Tao House 2, 11, 114, 127, 134, 135, 136, 139, 140–143, 162
Tao House Foundation 114
Taubman, Howard 37
Taylor, Robert 137
Tender Is the Night 159
Theatre-in-America 82
The Theatre Guild 23, 31, 72, 115
Theatre Hall of Fame 101
A Thousand Clowns 9, 56, 125, 148, 188
Time magazine 73
Tiusanen, Timo 108
Tone, Franchot 106
Tony Award 101, 109, 126, 146, 159, 160, 188
Torn, Rip 106
Törnqvist, Egil 108
A Touch of the Poet 10, 21, 66, 94, 103, 109, 110*n4*, 115, 125, 180, 188; aborted 1973 Theatre-in-America production 82; 1958 production 82, 106; 1977 production 82–91; O'Neill fails to produce 81; production history 91, 106
Toys in the Attic 56, 125
Turnbull, Andrew 146
Tracy, Spencer 81, 91
Travanti, Daniel 106
The Treasure of the Sierra Madre 29
Trinity Repertory Theatre (Providence, R.I.) 11
Twelfth Night 164

Ullmann, Liv 106, 107

Valentine, Dean 88
Vena, Gary 26*n2*
Venice Festival 106
Victoria Regina 16

Wagner, Richard 124
Wainscott, Ronald 23
Waldorf Astoria Hotel 159
Wallach, Eli 115, 195–197
Washburn, Jane Caldwell 129
Washington Times 97
Waterford, Connecticut 13
Waterston, Sam 106

Watts, Richard, Jr. 37
Wayne, David 106
Weales, Gerald 69
Weaver, Fritz 7
Wellington, Duke of 84, 88, 89, 91
Westwood Playhouse (Los Angeles)
Wheeler, Hugh 159
Where the Cross Is Made 110*n4*
White, George 13, 126, 143
Whitehead, Robert 82
Whiting, Margaret 106
Wilkins, Frederick 3, 180

Williams, Tennessee 113, 124, 167
Williamson, Nicol 147
Willson, Meredith 24–25
Wilson, Elizabeth 115, 159
Winther, Sophus Keith 107
Wolfson, Victor 171
Wolheim, Louis 68, 125, 126
Wright, Teresa 12, 16

Yale Repertory Theatre 143
Yerma 166
You Can't Take It with You 12